602

974.602

COLONIAL
Connecticut

Arthur E. Soderlind

THOMAS NELSON INC., PUBLISHERS
Nashville   New York

Photographs courtesy of the Connecticut State Library, with the exception of the following: pp. 59, 72, 95, 113, 119 from the Connecticut Historical Society; pp. 29, 34 from the author's collection; pp. 26, 56 from the First Church of Christ in Hartford. Permission is gratefully acknowledged.

Copyright © 1976 by Arthur E. Soderlind

All rights reserved under International and Pan-American Conventions. Published in Nashville, Tennessee, by Thomas Nelson Inc., Publishers, and simultaneously in Don Mills, Ontario, by Thomas Nelson & Sons (Canada) Limited. Manufactured in the United States of America.

First edition

Library of Congress Cataloging in Publication Data
Soderlind, Arthur E
   Colonial Connecticut.
   Bibliography: p.
   Includes index.
   SUMMARY: Traces Connecticut's history from its exploration and settlement by the Dutch in the seventeenth century to 1788, when it became the fifth state to ratify the Constitution.
   1. Connecticut—History—Colonial period, ca. 1600-1775—Juvenile literature. 2. Connecticut—History—Revolution, 1775-1783—Juvenile literature. [1. Connecticut—History—Colonial period, ca. 1600-1775. 2. Connecticut—History—Revolution, 1775-1783] I. Title.
F97.S62   974.6'02   76-3588
ISBN 0-8407-7136-3

Acknowledgments

I am indebted to Melancthon Jacobus of the Connecticut Historical Society; Barbara van der Lyke and David O. White of the State Library; and Olive Niles, Janet Meleney, and my wife for their help and encouragement. —A. E. S.

Qui Transtulit Sustinet
(He Who Transplanted Still Sustains)

To My Father
who was transplanted

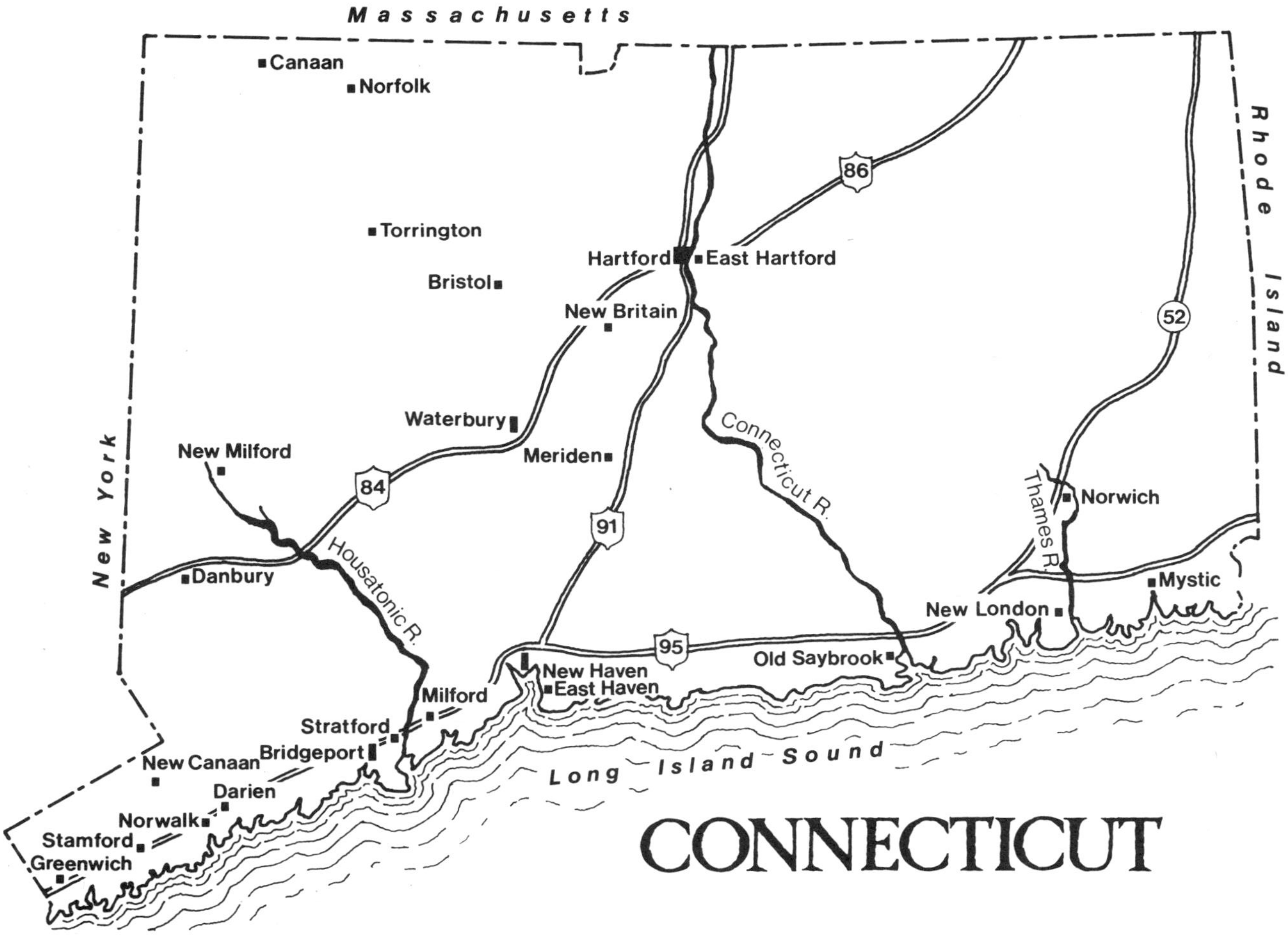

CONNECTICUT

Contents

1. By the Long Tidal River   9
2. The Transplanting   19
3. Establishing Roots   36
4. From Puritan to Yankee   49
5. The Royal Colony   62
6. The Land of Steady Habits   74
7. Prelude to the Revolution   89
8. The Colony Is Aroused   101
9. The Provision State   111
10. Connecticut Men at War   124
11. The Constitution State Joins the Union   138
    Important Dates   147
    Historic Sites   149
    Bibliography   153
    Index   155

Roger Sherman (1721–1793), a member of the First Continental Congress, was also a delegate to the Constitutional Convention in 1787. There, he and Oliver Ellsworth introduced the Connecticut Compromise, which proposed the dual system of representation existing in Congress today.

CHAPTER ONE

By the Long Tidal River

It must have been a warm, sunny day that May of 1614 when the *Onrust* sailed into the mouth of a river at a point now called Old Saybrook. The *Onrust*, a small craft even for those times, was only 44½ feet long with a beam of 11½ feet and a displacement of sixteen tons. Although the current was not strong in the shallow estuary at the mouth of the river, a fairly strong wind off Long Island Sound was needed to propel the tiny *Onrust* across the turbulence caused by the treacherous and shifting sandbar just below the surface of the water and to allow the small craft to sail up the river.

May in this area of New England was usually a month of bright sunlit days with high fluffy clouds floating lazily across the sky. Under these conditions the land heated up faster than the waters of the Sound, and the winds, constant and gentle, were generally from the south.

Navigating a small craft like the *Onrust* up the river against the current, and with the main channel constantly changing direction, required all the skill that Adriaen Block, the Dutch commander of the *Onrust*, and his crew possessed, so they had to divide their attention between the beauty of the countryside and the demands of the river. Mile after mile of broad meadows, marshes, and forested woodlands of oak, elm, maple, and flowering dogwood greeted them as they proceeded up the river. The depth of the water varied, in some places no more than five feet deep, but the favorable southerly winds enabled the *Onrust* to sail about sixty miles up the river to a point 41 degrees 48 minutes north latitude, just north of the present city of Hartford. The *Onrust* was unable to proceed any farther north because there the river became very shallow and had a rocky bottom.

Before being forced to turn back, Block and the crew made friends with the Indians living along the edge of the river and became aware of the possibilities of a lucrative fur trade. Block named the river the "Versche" or "Fresh Water" River because of the strong downward current of fresh water. However, this river eventually came to be known not by its Dutch name but by its Indian name, "Connecticut."

The Indians who populated the river valley belonged to the Algonkian family, and in their language, "Connecticut" was not a proper noun but a phrase: *Conne*, "long;" *tic*, "tidal river;" and *ut*, "by"—"by the long tidal river."

The Algonkian Family

The first red men to welcome the Dutch, the English, and the French in the New World belonged to the Algonkian nation. This great family of tribes ranged east of the Mississippi from Hudson's Bay on the north to Tennessee and Virginia on the south. They were highly self-sufficient; able to supply their own needs without coming into conflict with their surroundings.

They often came into conflict with one another, however. There were about a hundred Algonkian tribes, all independent and having divergent interests. In New England the more important tribes were the Penobscot, the Narragansett, the Pequot, the Massachset, the Wanpanoag, and the Mahican, or Mohegans. Quarreling and feuding was forever breaking out among them, usually because one aggressive tribe had invaded the territories of its neighbors.

The Pequots invaded Connecticut from the west—from the Hudson River Valley, it is believed, south of what is now Albany—not many years before the arrival of the white man. They encountered the Connecticut River Indians, the Podunks, in the area near the present city of Hartford and continued east into the land of the Nipmunks and the Narragansetts. In time the English came to call all these Indians by the name "Pequots," which means "destroyers of men."

A family of River Valley Indians, members of the Algonkian nation, prepare to greet the *Onrust*.

The internecine tribal feuding among the sixteen Algonkian tribes in Connecticut made them easy prey to the Dutch and English settlers. At the time of the arrival of the white man in Connecticut, the Indian population was perhaps only six or seven thousand. They lived mainly along the coast and in the central river valley, where they raised corn, beans, squash, and tobacco in the rich alluvial soil.

Life Among the River Valley Indians

Among the Algonkians in Connecticut corn ranked as the main source of food and was used in addition to the meat, fowl, and fish they caught in the nearby forests and rivers. The women tended the crops in the fields, but the men did nearly all the fishing, and they hunted and trapped the deer and other animals that provided both meat and skins for clothing. The men also protected their people against attack by hostile tribes.

In the forested areas wildlife was varied and plentiful. Deer, bear, raccoon, mink, otter, and fox roamed freely, easy prey to the wolf and wildcat. Turkey, heron, pigeon, partridge, and quail were likewise abundant.

The Indians' clothing was not elaborate. The women wore skirts made by folding a rectangular skin around the waist. Occasionally a woman formed deerhide into a crude jacket, which she wore as an upper garment. The men wore moccasins, leggings, breechcloths, and in colder weather, robes. Both men and women took good care of their hair, which was regularly dressed with bear fat to keep it glossy black. While the women wore theirs long, the men cut theirs short on the sides, leaving a cockscomb from the top of the head to the nape of the neck. This was frequently dressed with bits of shell, colored stones, or deer bristles (from the tail) dyed bright red.

They lived in wigwams—simple yet comfortable dwelling places that consisted of an oval framework of poles, bent into a dome shape and covered with slabs of elm bark or woven mats of grass. A fire was built in the center and provided with an escape hole in the roof, and platforms around the sides provided a sleeping and sitting space above the tamped-earth floor.

At the time of the arrival of the white man, the Algonkian mode of life was that of the Stone Age, for metal tools were unknown. Most household utensils were of bark or wood, reeds or wood splints.

The Physical Environment

The region, known today as the State of Connecticut, is divided roughly in half by the Connecticut River Valley. The central lowland separates the western uplands from the eastern uplands, each of which is cut up into many small river valleys and contains numerous lakes and ponds. In the western uplands the major rivers are the Housatonic and its largest tributary, the Naugatuck; in the east the major river is the Thames and its tributaries.

The rivers over the years not only provided a means of transportation and later waterpower; they were also an important source of food, for they teemed with fish, the salmon and the shad being the most important. All the rivers empty into Long Island Sound, whose northern shoreline contains many small harbors, coves, and islands. Along the shoreline shellfish, clams, oysters, and lobsters were abundant.

At the beginning of the seventeenth century, most of Connecticut was covered with virgin forests of hardwoods like ash, beech, birch, chestnut, elm, hickory, maple, oak, sycamore, and walnut and of softwoods like balsam, cedar, hemlock, and pine. These trees grew in profusion except for the flood plains and the small clearings made by the Indians. Most of the Indians lived on the high ground just above the flood plains, which were lush with grass in the summer and later provided a natural fodder for the cattle and livestock of the white settlers.

The climate of Connecticut was and still is mild, rarely very hot or very cold. The rainfall, distributed fairly evenly throughout the year, averages about forty-six inches; in fact, it is not unlike the climate of England from which most of the early settlers came.

Adriaen Block

In 1611 a group of Amsterdam merchants, excited by the news of Henry Hudson's discoveries in the *Half Moon,* chartered a vessel to make additional explorations of the Hudson River. Adriaen Block and his partner, Hendrick Christiaensen, were aboard this vessel. When it returned with a valuable cargo of fur pelts, the merchants saw the possibilities of a lucrative fur trade and thereupon agreed to finance two more ships—the *Tiger,* to be captained by Block, and the *Fortune,* by Christiaensen.

Both ships entered the placid harbor of what is now New York City, late in the summer of 1613. The *Tiger* anchored off Manhattan Island while the *Fortune* proceeded upstream to the Albany area. Bartering trifles with the Indians, Block soon had the *Tiger* loaded with beaver, otter, and other furs. However, a fire broke out on board and spread rapidly, and the ship burned to the water line. The vessel was a complete loss, although Block and the crew managed to salvage spare sails, rope, shipwright tools, and other fittings.

Almost immediately Block and the crew, with the help of friendly Indians, began to lay the keel of a new ship. The Indians, who supplied Block and his crew with dried meat, fish, and corn meal, also built crude huts which enabled the Europeans to survive the winter.

The *Onrust*

Late in the spring of 1614 Block's crew launched the new vessel, christened the *Onrust*, meaning "Restlessness," and sailed up the east side of Manhattan Island through the "Helle-gadt" or "Hell Gate," a treacherous tidal channel with swirling currents and hidden rocks, into Long Island Sound.

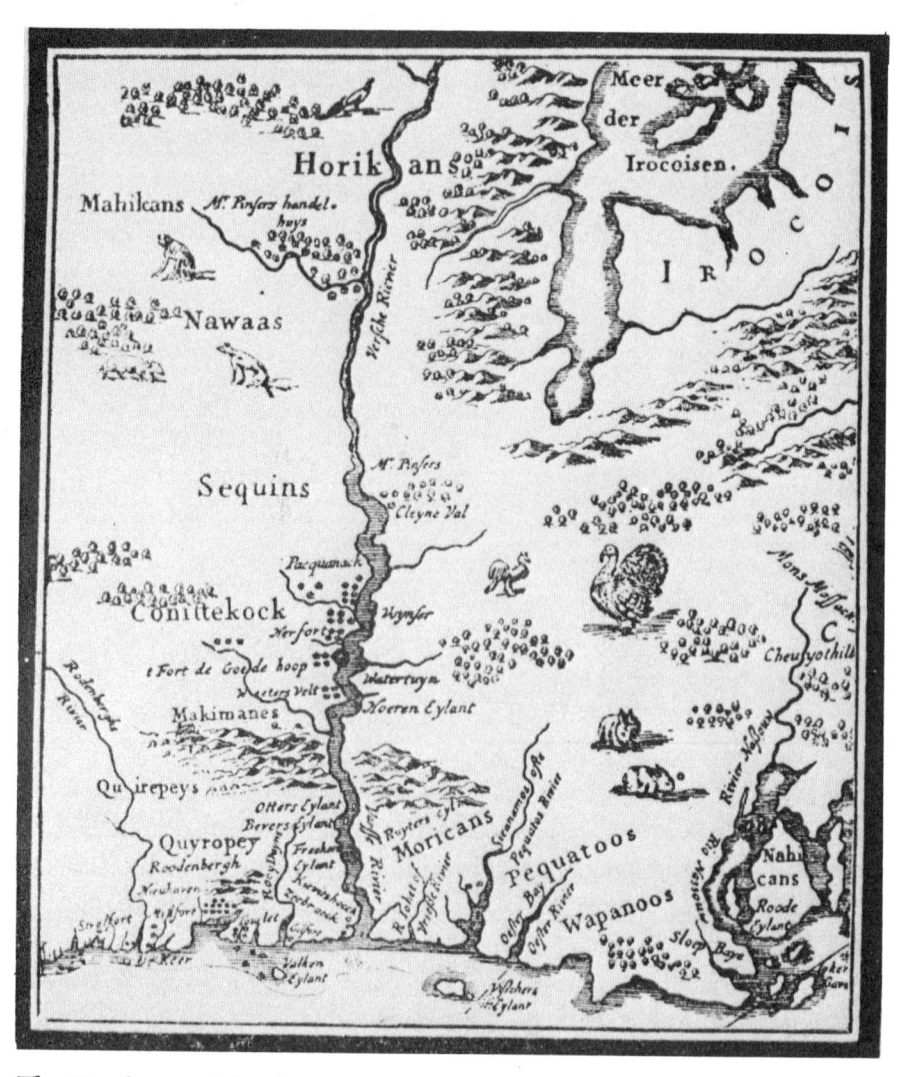

This Dutch map of the Connecticut River Valley shows not only the topography of the area, but also the animals found there.

The *Onrust* sailed eastward along the northern shore of "Groote" Bay, or the "Beautiful Inland Sea," while Block charted the coast's contours with its harbors, inlets, rivers, and islands. Later he described the mouth of the Housatonic River as being "a bow-shot wide," and impressed by the redness of the countryside, he named that area "Roodenbergen," or "Red Hills." Farther to the east, the present New Haven harbor was named the Harbor of Roodenbergen because of the red sandstone hills nearby.

After taking time to explore the Connecticut River, Block continued on an easterly course, charting the shore, until he anchored at the mouth of the "River of the Siccanams," or the Thames River. He then sailed southeast across the Sound to Montauk Point on Long Island and to Block Island, the only piece of land named in his memory.

Fully six years before the arrival of the Pilgrims on the *Mayflower*, Block explored Cape Cod and Plymouth Bay. He sailed to 42 degrees 30 minutes north latitude (roughly, modern Marblehead, Massachusetts) before he decided to return home to Holland and report his discoveries. Because the *Onrust* was too small for a safe return across the unpredictable Atlantic, Block knew he had to find the *Fortune*, which had been exploring the Hudson River. Happily the *Onrust* and the *Fortune* encountered one another near Cape Cod. Leaving one of the crew in command of the *Onrust*, Block directed him to continue to explore the general area, especially the region south of the Hudson River.

While Block was exploring and mapping the coastline of Long Island Sound and Cape Cod and establishing claims for Holland, an Englishman, Captain John Smith, was also exploring and mapping the New England coast and establishing claims for England. Neither of them knew of the activities of the other.

The United New Netherland Company

Upon their return to Holland in July 1614, Block and Christiaensen found that fevered interest in the area of the Hudson River had prompted the States-General (legislature) of the Dutch Republic in March to allow the original investors the profits and discoveries of the first six voyages to New Netherland. These original investors formed the United New Netherland Company and sent out five ships between 1611 and 1614 to the general region of 40 degrees north latitude.

To assist in these voyages and later settlement, a skilled cartographer was employed to draw a "Figurative Map," under Block's supervision, based on the charting and data collected by the *Onrust's* crew. Block's descriptions of the discoveries in Long Island Sound and up the Connecticut River caused the States-General to grant "a charter for exclusive trading privileges in the region represented on the Figurative Map." This charter granted the United New Netherland Company a trade monopoly in "Nieuw Nederlandt," a territory between 40 degrees and 45 degrees north latitude, or between the claims of the English in Virginia to the south and of the French in Canada to the north. However, the terms of the charter limited the company to only four voyages over a period of three years from January 1, 1615.

During the next three years no permanent settlements were made, although the fur trade continued to be profitable. When the charter expired in 1618, the States-General refused to renew it for the exclusive use of the United New Netherland Company and decided to allow "all inhabitants" of the United Dutch Provinces the right to trade in New Netherland. As a result, trading increased. Merchants loaded ships with trinkets and trifles for bartering with the Indians and in return received cargoes of fine furs.

The Dutch Settlements

In March 1624 a group of thirty families, mostly Belgian Walloons who were unhappy under Dutch rule, sailed from Amsterdam on the *Nieuw Nederlandt* to settle in the New World. After the safe arrival of the ship in New Amsterdam harbor at the lower tip of Manhattan in May, eight of the families settled in the area of Manhattan Island and the East River, two settled on the South, or Delaware River, two on the banks of the lower Connecticut River, and the rest up the Hudson River just south of the present city of Albany. When the *Nieuw Nederlandt* returned to Holland in the fall of 1624, the captain reported the colonists happily settled in their new homes and having friendly relations with the Indians. However, the families who settled at what is now Saybrook Point at the mouth of the Connecticut River were not so comfortable as reported. They endured the loneliness of their situation for two years, then joined the others at New Amsterdam.

According to the Dutch records, Woopigwooit, the great chief, or sachem, of the Pequots, sold the lands at Saybrook and Hartford to the first Dutch settlers, even though the Podunks were the rightful owners of the Connecticut River Valley lands. In 1632 Governor Wouter Van Twiller of New Amsterdam took possession of a point of land at the mouth of the Connecticut River in the name of Holland by nailing the Dutch coat of arms to a tree. This place was called Kievit's Hook. The Dutch planned to build a fort and so control the river and valley.

In June of the following year Jacob Van Curler arrived at the site of the present city of Hartford with a party of men to establish a trading post. He purchased from Woopigwooit a piece of land approximately one mile long and one third of a mile wide, for which he paid "1 piece of duffel 27 ells long, 6 axes, 6 kettles, 18 knives, one sword blade, 1 pr. of shears, some toys and a musket." Upon this site Van Curler built a small fort, mounted two cannon in it and called it the House of [Good] Hope. All the Indians in the area were encouraged to trade there, and for a time the hatchet was buried among the rival tribes, for no warrior was to harm his enemy within sight of the trading fort.

The English Toehold

In 1631, two years before Van Curler's arrival in the Hartford area, a group of Connecticut River Indians, who had been defeated in a battle with the Pequots, visited the English at Plymouth and Boston to urge them to come to Connecticut. They described the river valley as a beautiful and fertile country abounding in fish, game, and fur-bearing animals and begged the Massachusetts Bay colonists to make settlements there.

In the summer of 1632 Edward Winslow of Plymouth sailed up the Connecticut River to confirm the Indians' statements. He got as far north as the present site of Windsor, north of Hartford, where he purchased some land from the local Indians. The following year, the Plymouth Colony sent out William Holmes to this region. As his ship sailed past the House of Hope, he was challenged by the Dutch, but no shots were fired. At the Windsor site, Holmes and his crew erected a house frame, which they had carried from Plymouth aboard their vessel. Around the building they hurriedly built a palisade, or stockade, as a protection from

William Holmes sailed past the Dutch Fort of Good Hope on his way to settle the English town of Windsor.

both the Indians and the Dutch. Thus, the town of Windsor was established.

One month later seventy Dutch soldiers were sent to Windsor to drive Holmes and his settlers out of the Connecticut Valley. The Dutch demanded "that he depart forthwith, with all his people and houses." However, Holmes refused, and the Dutch commander, deciding the situation was not serious enough for a fight, returned to the fort.

In the end, the newcomers were to outlast the Dutch, for the latter eventually abandoned the House of Hope and returned to New Amsterdam.

CHAPTER TWO

The Transplanting

The waves of religious reform set in motion by the Protestant Reformation reached England a generation or so after Martin Luther nailed his ninety-five theses to the church door in Wittenberg. Conditions in England were favorable for a revolt against the Roman Catholic Church. A growing sense of national unity had been fermenting in England since the late Middle Ages, and during the last quarter of the fifteenth century under Henry VII, the first Tudor king, England became a nation in the modern sense of the word.

During the reign of Henry VIII, the formal break with the Church of Rome took place, and the Church of England was established with Henry as its titular head. In the years after Henry VIII's death in 1547, the Protestants and the Catholics challenged each other for control of the government.

First, Henry's young son, Edward VI, ruled for six years with Protestant advisers. Then, he died of consumption, and Henry's older daughter, Mary, brought the Catholics back into power for another five years. She was known as Bloody Mary, because she ordered the persecution and death of some three hundred of the more prominent Protestant "heretics" in the interests of reestablishing the Roman Church.

The Reign of Elizabeth I

When Henry's third child, Elizabeth, came to the throne in 1558, England once more had a Protestant monarch. Elizabeth, known as the

Virgin Queen because she never married, reigned for forty-five magnificent years. The Age of Elizabeth was one of the most glorious periods in English history—a prosperous time during which the theater, the arts, literature, education, and commerce flourished, and the old medieval ways and customs gave way to a new order called the English Renaissance.

England was becoming the most powerful and important nation in Europe. By the early 1600's the population in England passed the four million mark, and the economic well-being of the people reached new highs.

The sea voyages of John Cabot, Sir Francis Drake, Sir Martin Frobisher, and others during the fifteenth and sixteenth centuries established claims for England in the New World. Elizabeth's encouragement of overseas trading companies built up a strong merchant marine. The English sea captains did everything they could to harass and ravage the trade of the Spanish and the Dutch. After the defeat of the Spanish Armada in 1588, the influence of the English steadily increased while the power, fortunes, and empire of the Spanish declined. As a result, surplus wealth developed, and the English people had money to invest in overseas ventures.

The religious differences between the Catholics and the Protestants, however, were not settled during Elizabeth's long reign. Because she was a very shrewd politician, she usually chose a middle-of-the-road religious position, but the forces set in motion by the Reformation were too powerful to be settled without conflict. Reformers became a strong element in the religious and social life of England, and their teachings and influence spread far and wide.

The English reformers were divided into three groups. The Presbyterians followed the teaching of John Calvin. Their main strength was in Scotland, and they carried the Reformation even further from the doctrines of the Catholic Church than the Lutherans did by following Calvin's ideas on church government and the doctrine of the divine predestination of every human being to a state of bliss in Heaven after death or of damnation in Hell. The Brownists or Separatists included the Pilgrims of Plymouth Rock fame and were later known as Congregationalists because they advocated the independence of each individual congregation or church. The largest group, who wished to stay within the Church of England and "purify or reform" it, were known simply as Puritans.

The Puritans sought to return the Church to the "purity" of its early

Christian years. They felt their religious beliefs developed through an experience of conversion, or rebirth, which separated them from other worshipers and gave them the benefits and responsibilities of God's love. This conversion often came about from hearing a fervent sermon. The Puritans placed a great deal of emphasis on the sermon. They held ideals of strict piety or godliness in their everyday life and desired to create "a godly and righteous nation."

During the last years of Elizabeth's reign, the Puritans lost favor with the government and actually suffered many persecutions. With Elizabeth's death in 1603 and the passing of the throne to James I, the Puritans felt that perhaps they would receive a more favorable treatment. However, their demands for reform within the Church of England were rejected. Under James's son, Charles I, life for the Puritans in England became almost unbearable. Many of the more committed emigrated to Protestant Holland, but its foreign ways were not to their liking. As a result, most of them, especially those who had been in the most trouble with the government, decided to make a fresh start in the New World.

Thomas Hooker

In this social and religious environment Thomas Hooker, one of the founders of Connecticut, grew to manhood. He was born in 1586 in the quiet little hamlet of Marefield in the midlands of England, not far from where William Shakespeare, John Bunyan, and Oliver Cromwell were born. Very little is known of his early life, but as a boy of thirteen or fourteen Hooker was sent to Bosworth Grammar School, where he learned his Latin and Greek. At eighteen he enrolled in Queen's College and later in Emmanuel College, at Cambridge University, then "the intellectual nurseries of the Puritan Party in England."

Cambridge in those years seethed with new and dissenting ideas, beliefs, and practices. The young and receptive Hooker found the campus stimulating, as did many other religious leaders who were to be prominent later in the founding and development of New England.

Hooker probably left Cambridge in 1620, the year the Pilgrims landed at Plymouth, and became a minister in a little country church about sixteen miles from the center of London. Later he became a lecturer in St.

Mary's Church, Chelmsford, Essex. During his four-year stay at Chelmsford, Hooker, a powerful and gifted preacher, made a deep impression upon the people of the region. They flocked from all directions to hear his exciting and unusual sermons. Even persons of high rank like the Earl of Warwick were drawn by Hooker's preaching. He also won over many of the irreligious, who had come originally to jeer and create disturbances.

Hooker's impassioned sermons on the vital subjects of Puritanism—predestination and the nature of God's grace—and on the perils of England brought him eventually to the attention of the Bishop of London (and later Archbishop of Canterbury), William Laud. In those days, because the Church of England was established as the official state religion, with the king as its head, religious unorthodoxy was regarded as treason. Although Bishop Laud was angry over Hooker's nonconformism, the preaching on forbidden topics continued. Hooker was therefore forced to resign—in spite of the pleas of fifty of his fellow preachers, who said, "We all esteem and

This statue, situated in front of the Old State House in Hartford, is dedicated to the Reverend Thomas Hooker.

know the said Thomas Hooker to be for doctrine orthodox, for life and conversation honest and for his disposition, peaceful."

For a while Hooker taught school in a nearby village where John Eliot, who was later to become a famous missionary to the New England Indians, was his assistant. Hooker did not feel safe from his powerful enemies, however, and so, following the example of many other nonconformists, he went to Holland. In so doing he was lucky because one of the ministers who supported him was later "whipped, branded, his nostrils slit, and his ears cut." Punishments in seventeenth-century England were cruel and disfiguring.

For a number of years the leaders of the Massachusetts Bay Company had been urging Hooker and other Puritan refugees in Holland to emigrate to New England. Life in Protestant Holland had failed to provide the good life they sought. Although they appreciated the sanctuary offered by the hospitable Dutch, Hooker and other Englishmen were unhappy in a foreign land. So, in 1633 Hooker left Holland, and after spending a few fearful weeks in England, he, his family, and many of his former congregation set sail aboard the *Griffin* for the uncertainties of the New World.

Aboard the ship also were John Haynes, Samuel Stone, and John Cotton. John Haynes was to become the first governor of Connecticut, John Cotton one of the religious leaders of the Massachusetts Bay Colony, and Samuel Stone, Hooker's associate in Hartford.

After eight long and harrowing weeks at sea, the *Griffin* arrived in Boston. Hooker and his party, assigned by the colony to New Town (now Cambridge), found their arrival a source of great rejoicing, the people saying that "their necessities were now supplied, for they had Cotton for their clothing, Hooker for their fishing, and Stone for their building."

Life in New Town proved to be everything except what Hooker and his friends had expected. Too many strong personalities resided in the small community. It was inevitable that clashes of opinion over religious and other differences would develop. The percentage of college graduates to the total population was probably the highest it has ever been in our history. Many, Hooker included, became dissatisfied with the Bay Colony leadership and methods of government. Hearing stories about the fertile

Connecticut River Valley to the west, they petitioned the General Court for permission to move, and were granted it.

So, shortly after Hooker's arrival at New Town, a group of men set out to explore the Connecticut River Valley with the intention of establishing settlements there.

The Migrations to the Three River Towns

John Oldham, who had visited the Hartford area in 1633, traveled with "The Ten Adventurers" and settled in Wethersfield. This settlement and the ones at Hartford and Windsor increased in size and number during the summer of 1635 as new groups arrived from the Bay Colony, "coming almost daily, some by water and some by land."

In late October 1635 a group of sixty people, men, women, and children, arrived at Hartford from New Town under the leadership of John Steele. They had traveled overland, a hundred miles through the wilderness with only a compass to guide them. They made the journey in two weeks on foot, following Indian trails and driving their livestock before them. Because of the absence of roads, most of their household goods and other provisions were to be brought from Boston up the Connecticut River by ship.

This band of courageous pioneers had scarcely settled in their new quarters when an early winter set in. The river became frozen and the expected provisions, like the extra food, clothing, and household goods, which had also been sent by boat, failed to arrive because the vessels were either wrecked or forced by storms to turn back to Boston. By December, as food supplies began to run low, conditions were desperate. Some corn was purchased from the meager supplies of the friendly Indians, but it was not enough to see them through the winter. Therefore, some of them, joined by others from Wethersfield and Windsor, returned overland through the deep snows to the Boston area, while another group—about seventy men, women, and children—went down the river in hopes of meeting the supply ships.

When they arrived at Saybrook, they found that the boats from Boston were not there. Luckily they were able to board another ship, the *Rebecca,* which was temporarily frozen in the ice of the river. A brief thaw and some

"He who brought us here sustains us still." The faith of the early settlers helped them in the difficult first years.

warm rains freed the ship, so that the half-starved families were able to return to Boston.

The hardy few who stayed on at the Three River Towns lived as the Indians did, and although often hungry and sickly, they survived the winter.

With the coming of spring, the hardships and sufferings of the winter were forgotten. Many who had fled to Massachusetts returned, bringing others with them, like Thomas Hooker and his entire congregation of more than one hundred. The elder John Winthrop made the following entry in his *Journal,* dated May 31, 1636:

> Mr. Hooker, pastor of the church of New Town and most of his congregation, went to Connecticut. His wife was carried in a horse-litter; and they drove one hundred and sixty cattle, and fed of their milk by the way.

Their journey, led by persons who had made the trip the year before, also took two weeks, as they drove this 160 head of cattle and a large

Thomas Hooker and his congregation, disenchanted with the autocratic government of Massachusetts, emigrated to Connecticut in 1636.

A frontal view of Thomas Hooker's house in Hartford, drawn shortly before it was torn down.

number of hogs "over mountains, through swamps and thickets" and across rivers "which were not passable save with great difficulty." Mrs. Hooker, who was ill, was carried the entire way in her litter. Fortunately, the weather remained well-nigh perfect throughout the journey.

Hooker's migratory congregation, "a goodly company of the fine English stock, splendid material for colonization," were "persons of figure who had lived in England in honor, affluence, and delicacy, and were entire strangers to fatigue and danger." They sang psalms and made the woods ring with their shouting and laughter, because they were a happy group who enjoyed the walking, the sleeping under the stars, and the wading of the streams at the fords used by the Indians. They followed the old narrow, winding Indian trails, probably the Bay Path (roughly U.S. 20) westward and then the Old Connecticut Path (which followed a route slightly south of the present I-86) southwesterly, passing near the present towns of Woodstock, Mansfield, and Manchester until they reached the Connecticut River at Podunk (East Hartford). They settled near the Dutch fort, where others from the New Town area had settled.

Hartford, Wethersfield, and Windsor

Within a year after the arrival of Hooker's congregation, the population of the Three River Towns numbered a good eight hundred people. The land on the west bank of the Connecticut River had been parceled out in two-acre plots and in farm tracts, which were granted in size and value according to each individual's contributions in worldly goods and services or to family needs and claims to personal dignity. Each grant was to be improved within the year by having a dwelling built and the fields cleared and planted.

The first houses went up quickly. Plenty of lumber was available in the forested hills nearby, and grass for thatching grew thickly in the lush meadows along the river. These early thatched roofs were later replaced by shingle, because of the danger of fire from the chimneys. Large fireplaces of locally made brick or fieldstone, used for both cooking and heating, were the focal points of all houses.

The kitchen fireplace was the center of an early home. It was always large, up to nine feet wide, and sometimes built with seats at the sides, so that children could sit close to the center of heat and watch the sparks fly up the throat of the chimney. At the back of the fireplace, resting on ledges projecting from the stone, was the "back bar"—a stout pole of green wood, from which the cooking pots were hung on chains or hooks. In time this back bar would become charred through, and there would be a mighty crash as bar, pots, kettles, food, and all came thundering down into the fire. Later back bars were made of iron, and later still they were replaced with swinging cranes, from which hung "trammels" (jagged-edged pot hooks, which could be adjusted to hold the cooking pot at any height).

Most of the cooking was done directly over the flame in a large kettle or on a spit. Dogs were sometimes used to operate treadmills that kept the spit rotating at an even speed. Baking was done either in a brick oven or in a bake kettle. Oven baking was a laborious, all-day chore, in which the cook built a fire inside the oven and kept it going until the bricks reached the proper temperature—tested usually by her own skilled hand—then raked out coals and embers and put in the risen bread. Correctly fired, the bricks retained heat for hours, ample time to bake the loaves.

Baking in a kettle was easier. The kettle was a broad, low, heavy vessel, raised up on legs and equipped with a heavy lid that sat well inside the lip of the bottom part. The dough or batter was placed inside this kettle, the lid was replaced, and hot coals or embers were laid on top (the protruding lip kept them in place). Then it was placed on its legs over a low fire for half an hour or so, while the dough baked from both top and bottom. As a rule, yeast bread was baked in the oven, quick breads, such as muffins, biscuits, and popovers, in the kettle.

The kitchen fireplace was usually part of a central chimney built in the middle of the house with rooms around it. These rooms contained fireplaces that were also part of the central chimney. Houses built later sometimes had fireplaces at either end of the house. In winter the fireplaces provided the only warmth and light in the house, because colonial houses did not have central heating or large windows. On cold days and evenings this warmth barely extended beyond three feet from the fireplace, so the rest of the room remained cold and cheerless. Early diaries report ink freezing in the inkwell, wash water freezing on the bedside stand. Courting couples were tucked up in bed, the bundling board between them, to whisper and flirt without suffering chilblains. Fireside seats were built with high straight backs to shield against icy drafts.

The Henry Whitfield House (built 1639) in Guilford is the oldest stone house in New England.

The family lived for the most part in the kitchen, where the social life of the people appeared in its most pleasant form. On the long winter evenings the family gathered around the large fireplace, where the children received instruction in their Bible studies. Because there was no place in early Connecticut for idle hands or minds, everyone kept busy with lap chores—knitting, sewing, whittling, making brooms. Not infrequently the sober reading of Bible passages was interrupted by the merry laughter of children.

The Reverend Mr. Hooker's Famous Sermon

During the first years, the distant General Court of Massachusetts ruled the settlers of the Three River Towns. However, many of these people had left Massachusetts for the very reason that they disliked the Bay Colony government, so it soon became necessary to establish their own form of government. The earliest town meeting was held in 1635, and the first General Court of the Three River Towns was held on April 6, 1636, before the arrival of the Hooker congregation. At another meeting of the General Court on May 1, 1637, representatives of the Three Towns met in Hartford. They included six magistrates and nine "committees," or representatives.

By 1638 this simple system no longer worked well for the three fast-growing towns. Because these representatives were able to choose the magistrates and could therefore perpetuate themselves in office, Hooker and others felt that a change was necessary. On May 31, 1638, he preached a famous sermon, which led to the writing of the Fundamental Orders of Connecticut.

Speaking mainly to the members of the General Court, Hooker took for his text Deuteronomy 1:13: "Take you wise men, and understanding, and known among your tribes, and I will make them rulers over you." Like Moses of old, Hooker proclaimed three doctrines:

> 1. That the choice of public magistrates belongs unto the people by God's own allowance.
> 2. The privilege of election which belongs unto the people must not be exercised according to their humour, but according to the blessed will of God.
> 3. That they who have the power to appoint officers and magistrates, it is in their power also to set the bounds of the power and place unto which they call them.

In other words, (1) the people have the God-given right to appoint their own public officers; (2) the people ought to do this thoughtfully and in the fear of God; and (3) the people who appoint the officers should set the limits of the power and duties of the officers they choose.

Hooker believed in two important doctrines: first, that the true authority for a government is "the free consent of the people," and secondly, that the people are more apt to obey their rulers if they have been given the free opportunity to choose them. He argued not for a democratic government, where all men are equal, but for a fixed code of laws the magistrates would use in their actions.

Roger Ludlow

Thomas Hooker may have formulated the doctrines that became the Fundamental Orders of Connecticut, but the actual wording of the document shows the hand of someone trained for the law. It is generally assumed that Roger Ludlow authored the Fundamental Orders.

Ludlow, born in 1590 to a distinguished family in England, attended Balliol College at Oxford University, where he was an outstanding student in both his academic and legal studies. His skill as a lawyer was based on his proficiency in the principles, forms, and precedents of legal procedure.

He emigrated to New England at the age of forty and soon became a leader of the Massachusetts Bay Colony. His specialty was interpreting the powers and authorities granted by the king's charter. After a couple of years, however, he became dissatisfied with the authoritarianism of the Bay Colony government, and along with Thomas Hooker and others, he looked to the west where "the civil rights of the common man were not subject to the dictates of wealth or the dominance of the church."

Shortly after arriving in the Three River Towns, Ludlow influenced the laws and rules governing the day-to-day life of the people. Being the only trained lawyer in those settlements, he established a court in May 1637. By the general consent of the people, he was made the presiding judge.

The Fundamental Orders

On January 14, 1639, the General Court of the Three Towns voted to adopt the Fundamental Orders, which consisted of an introduction and eleven "orders," as the basis for the government of Hartford, Wethersfield, and Windsor. The preamble stated that those towns joined together so that "there should be an Orderly and decent Gouerment established according to God to Order and dispose of the affayres of the people at all seasons as occation shall require."

The Fundamental Orders of Connecticut became the model for all the written constitutions later adopted in the United States, for it expressed five basic ideas that have become part of the inherent heritage of all "free Men":

1. All the authority of government comes directly from the people.
2. There shall be no taxation without representation.
3. The number of men that the town shall choose to help make their laws shall be in proportion to the population of the town.
4. All freemen who take an oath to be faithful to the State shall have the right to vote.

5. New Towns may join the three original towns and live under the same government.

The Orders called also for the General Court, the legislative body of the colony, to meet twice a year, in April and September. At the April meeting, the Court chose a governor and six magistrates on an annual basis, and no person could serve as governor more than once in two years. Furthermore, the governor had to belong to "some approved congregation" and to have served as a magistrate.

Each of the Three Towns elected four representatives to the General Court, and any towns that joined in the future would have the numbers of their representatives determined by the Court. No religious qualifications were required. The governor and the magistrates, together with the representatives of the towns, transacted all business that concerned the colony as a whole, but each town had absolute control of its local affairs. Furthermore, if the governor or the magistrates failed to perform their duties or attempted to misuse their authority, a majority of the freemen might call together a new General Court, without the governor or the magistrates, and elect a new moderator to preside. Thus the ultimate power of government lay with the people, and they had the right to decide how they were to be governed. "The People" were the government and the government was based on the principles of justice and righteousness, "according to the laws here established and for want thereof according to the Word of God."

On the second Tuesday of April 1639, the Fundamental Orders went into effect when the "admitted inhabitants" and the "freemen," that is the qualified voters, of the Three Towns met in Hartford and elected John Haynes the first governor and Roger Ludlow the first deputy governor of Connecticut.

Fort Saybrook

In 1632 two noblemen, Lord Brooke and Lord Say and Sele, formed a company of noted English gentlemen dissatisfied with the religious and political affairs of their day. The Saybrook Company, as it was later called, received from the Earl of Warwick on March 19 a grant of all land "which lies west from the Narragansett River, a hundred and twenty miles on the coast, and from there in latitude and breadth aforesaid to the South Sea." Whether the earl had the legal right to make this grant has been questioned. However, since he was the president of the Council of Plymouth and that council was "the mother of all land grants in New England," deriving its authority from Charles I, Warwick was, no doubt, acting in good faith in making the grant to his friends and business associates. If the terms of the Warwick Patent had remained in effect, the founders of Saybrook would have controlled the area from Rhode Island to the Pacific Ocean.

But the settlement of Saybrook at the mouth of the Connecticut River failed to realize the dreams of its founders. During the 1630's political conditions in England changed rapidly, and the Puritan "men of quality" who had planned to emigrate to the New World and settle at Saybrook came to power in the 1640's and therefore remained in England.

The English take delight in tearing down the Dutch coat of arms and in renaming the site Saybrook in honor of Lord Say and Sele and Lord Brooke.

Lion Gardiner helped construct Fort Saybrook. His son was the first white child born in Connecticut.

In July 1635, Lord Say and Sele, Lord Brooke, and their associates appointed John Winthrop, Jr., the son of the governor of Massachusetts, as their agent in the New World. Winthrop, then visiting in England, received a commission to lay out and build a settlement suitable as a new home for these Puritan men of quality. Furthermore, he was designated as the "Governor of the River Connecticut" for a year.

When he returned to Boston in October, Winthrop heard rumors that the Dutch planned to build a fort at the mouth of the Connecticut River on the land they had purchased from the Indians in 1632. However, as we have seen, after nailing their coat of arms to a tree and naming the place Kievit's Hook, the Dutch had abandoned the area. Therefore, Winthrop hastened to begin his assignment of building a settlement. He and a crew of twenty had barely established the earthworks for a fort when a

Dutch vessel appeared at the mouth of the river, but at the sight of the English flag and the two mounted cannon, the ship withdrew and returned to New Amsterdam. When the fort was completed near the tree where the Dutch coat of arms was affixed, it was named Fort Saybrook, in honor of the two peers, Lord Say and Sele and Lord Brooke.

A civil and military engineer, Lieutenant Lion Gardiner, helped in the building of the fort, and he was placed in command upon its completion. Of his early experiences, Gardiner wrote:

> In the year of our Lord 1635, July the 10th, came I, Lion Gardiner, and Mary my wife, from Holland to London, and thence to New England, and dwelt at Saybrook Fort four years, of which I was commander; and there was born unto me a son named David, in 1636, April the 29th, the first born in that place. And then I went to Gardiner's Island which I bought of the Indians for ten coats of trading cloth.

Thus David Gardiner was the first white child born not only in Saybrook but in all of Connecticut.

John Winthrop, Jr., remained only a few weeks at Fort Saybrook, the hundreds of people scheduled to come from England never came, and so Saybrook failed to become the Puritan "city of refuge" for the persecuted of the English Civil War.

CHAPTER THREE

Establishing Roots

Initial relations between Indians and whites in Connecticut were friendly, but inevitably the time came when there was trouble. As increasing numbers of whites moved westward from Massachusetts to Connecticut, they showed greater and greater greed, violence, and duplicity in acquiring favorable farming land. To the Indians, all whites represented a threat to their lands, and although the Dutch were more interested in trading than in settling, the Indians made no distinction between them and the English.

The Indians could not understand the European concept of land ownership by individuals. They saw the land as something to be owned in common and used for the good of all, like the air. When the tillage around their own villages became depleted, the Indians simply moved on to a new site, and the land was allowed to return to its natural state. They assumed that white men would do the same, and when they "sold" the land, they thought they were merely renting its use for a limited period of time.

For years the various tribes of Connecticut Indians had warred upon each other. In 1633 the Pequots, the terror of all the other tribes, killed a few Indians who had been befriended by the Dutch at the House of Hope. When the Dutch retaliated by having the Pequot sachem Woopigwooit killed, the Pequots in turn sought ways to get revenge. Thus the smoldering rivalry between Sassacus, Woopigwooit's son and heir, and Uncas of the Mohegans, a friend of the whites, broke into open rebellion, with Uncas being defeated and forced to seek refuge among the Narragansetts of Rhode Island.

Sassacus represented the "noble savage," as that term was used by the early settlers and later historians. He was proud and intractable and "noted for prowess in war and wisdom in council. . . ." At one time he had supreme command over twenty-six other sachems, and "with regal authority [he] administered justice, punished rebels, and sent his ambassadors scores of miles demanding tribute. . . ." Early he realized the threat of the white man and began to devise means to curtail their settlements in his lands. The members of his tribe lived mainly along the coast of Long Island Sound, and from his headquarters on a section of elevated land between the Thames and the Mystic Rivers, he had a magnificent view of both the Atlantic and the Sound.

During the summer of 1634 the Pequots murdered Captain John Stone and eight men from Massachusetts who had come to trade. The initial encounter with the Indians was friendly enough, but Captain Stone, "a dissolute and intemperate man," who had left Virginia in disgrace, unwisely used firewater in his negotiations, and drink drove the Indians to murder.

In the aftermath of this incident, which Sassacus disclaimed, the Massachusetts authorities demanded that the murderers be turned over to them. The Indians did not comply, and relations between the two races were strained. Then in 1636, some other Indians killed John Oldham, one of the founders of Wethersfield, on Block Island.

The Massachusetts government thereupon sent a force of ninety men under the command of John Endicott to Block Island to avenge Oldham's death and to find the murderers of Stone. There turned out to be only a few Indians on Block Island, but Endicott's men nevertheless burned their village, destroyed their corn crop, and punched holes in their canoes. The Massachusetts men then crossed over to the Thames River on the Connecticut shore and met with representatives of the Pequots. Endicott told them what he and his men had done on Block Island as a punishment for the murder of Oldham and demanded that the murderers of Stone and the others be turned over to him. He also demanded twenty children as hostages. Instead, the Indians first attempted to jump Endicott and then fled.

Endicott and his troops then sailed to Fort Saybrook, where Lion Gardiner tried in vain to stop them from continuing their attacks on the

Pequots. He told them, "You have come to raise a nest of hornets about our ears, and then you will flee away." Endicott failed to take his advice and continued to destroy Indian villages along the shore before returning to Massachusetts. This, as Gardiner was well aware, only served to arouse the anger of the Pequots against the English.

During the winter of 1636–37 the Pequots laid siege to Fort Saybrook and killed nine of the garrison. In April the Pequots also raided the settlement of Wethersfield, killed six men and three women, destroyed cattle, and carried off two young girls as captives. With the captive girls plainly visible, the war party paddled down the river in their canoes past Fort Saybrook. Gardiner fired upon them, but the Indians escaped unharmed to return to their headquarters on the Thames River.

The Wethersfield girls, captured by Pequot Indians during a raid, cry for help as they are paddled past the fort at Saybrook.

The Pequot War

The Connecticut colonists were now aroused. On May 1, 1637, the General Court meeting in Hartford ordered an offensive against the Pequots. It raised an army of ninety men from the Three River Towns: forty-two from Hartford, thirty from Windsor, and eighteen from Wethersfield. These numbers were based on the population of the towns, and the towns also provided supplies according to their size. Captain John Mason, a resident of Windsor, commanded this small army.

Mason had considerable experience as a soldier. Before emigrating to New England, he had trained in the wars in the Netherlands. During the winter of 1637 he had been with Lion Gardiner at Fort Saybrook.

Accompanied by Uncas and seventy Mohegan and River Indians, Mason and his forces sailed down the river from Hartford on board three small ships. The wily Uncas and the Mohegans were more than willing to join the expedition because they saw it as an opportunity to get at their rivals, the Pequots. Upon arriving at Saybrook, they found the Wethersfield girls had been rescued by a Dutch trading vessel. From the girls Mason learned that the Pequots had sixteen guns but little powder.

Knowing that the Indians would expect them to attack from the west, Mason decided to sail as far east as Point Judith (near modern Narragansett, Rhode Island) and approach the main Pequot camp from the east through Narragansett country. To do this he naturally needed the cooperation of the Narragansett Indians, who were also enemies of the Pequots and gladly agreed. Two hundred of their warriors joined the expedition.

Marching back swiftly, the troops now numbering several hundred, Mason came to the Mystic River, near which two Pequot towns slumbered. He did not feel strong enough to attack both strongholds at the same time and concentrated instead on one. It was a brilliant moonlit night. Under Mason's directions, the attackers crept up silently and surrounded the palisaded village. By the time the alarm was given, it was too late. Mason ordered the village burned, and anyone who tried to escape from the holocaust was run down and slain.

Most of the Pequots died in the flames—about four hundred of them, warriors, women, old men, and children. Only seven were taken prisoner, and about an equal number escaped. Mason lost two killed and twenty wounded.

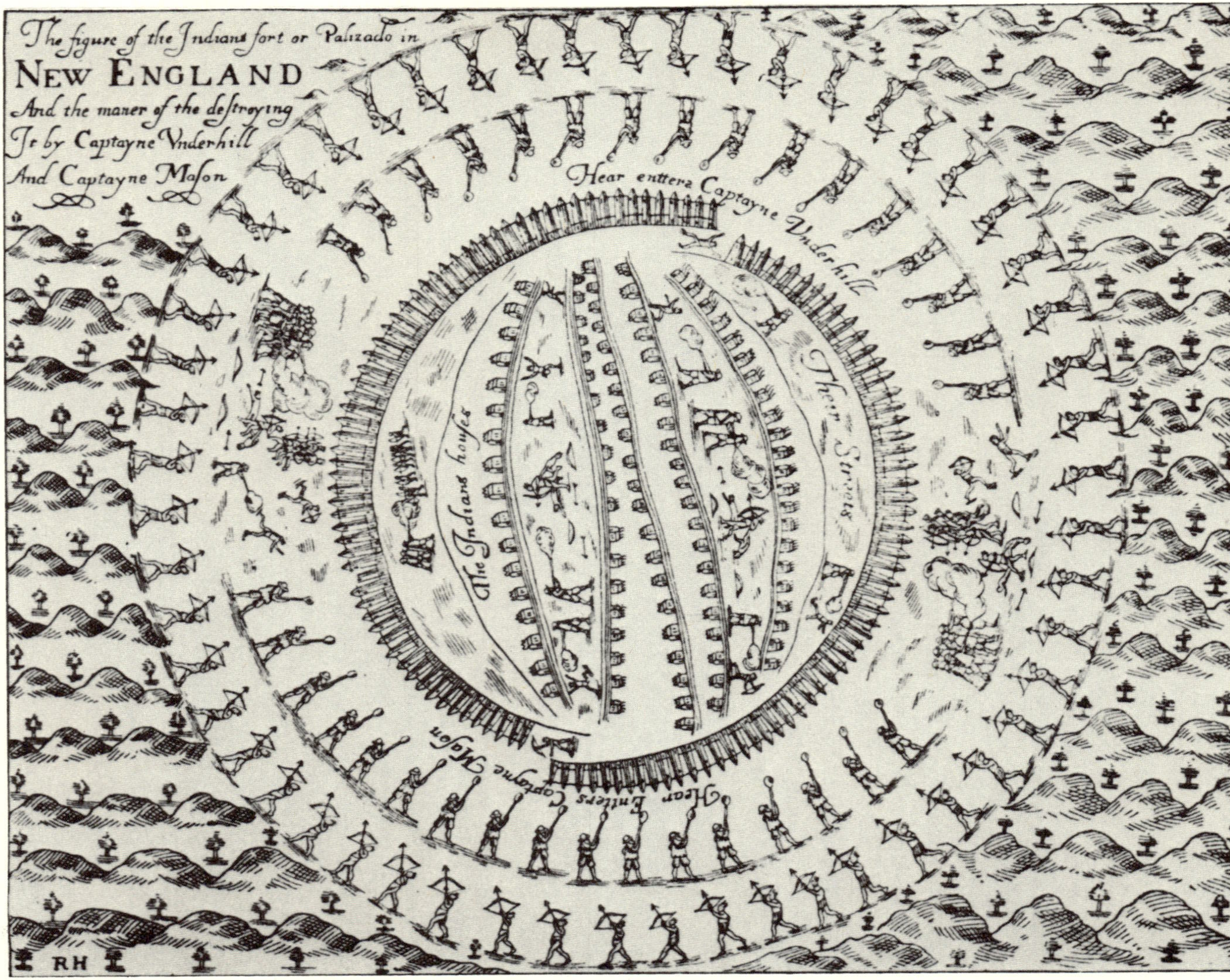

The figure of the Indians fort or Palizado in
NEW ENGLAND
And the maner of the destroying
It by Captayne Vnderhill
And Captayne Mason
Hear enttera Captayne Vnderhill
Their Streets
The Indians houses
Hear Entters Captayne Mason
RH

A group of about three hundred Pequot reinforcements under the command of Sassacus arrived about an hour after the battle. But their bows and arrows were no match for the guns of the English, who managed to kill or wound about one hundred of these men, too, before sailing away.

The Flight of the Pequots

The story of the white man's deeds spread rapidly among the remaining Pequots and the other Indian tribes. The Pequots decided to migrate west along the coast beyond Saybrook. At the Connecticut River they came upon three Englishmen and killed them as a parting insult and challenge to the English. The Pequots continued to flee westward and finally took refuge in a swamp near the present town of Fairfield.

The colonists, seeing the extermination of the Pequots as "the Lord's doings," were determined to pursue them. They tracked down the Pequots in the swamp and those who were not killed were taken captive. In this accomplishment the colonists saw an example of the Biblical verses, "Thus did the Lord scatter His enemies with His strong arm," and "Thus the Lord was pleased to smite our enemies and to give us their land for an inheritance."

The defeat of the Pequots had a great influence upon Connecticut history because it was to be thirty-six years, until the time of King Philip's War, before any Indian tribe made war again upon the white settlers. During those years the settlers firmly established their roots in the soil of Connecticut.

John Davenport

John Davenport was to the New Haven Colony what Thomas Hooker was to Hartford. In many ways their careers were similar and parallel, although Davenport was ten years younger than Hooker and a graduate of Oxford University rather than Cambridge.

Captain Mason led the attack on the Pequot fort. This midnight raid resulted in the destruction of the fort and the slaughter of most of its inhabitants.

Born in Coventry, Warwickshire, in 1597, the fifth son of prominent parents, Davenport entered Oxford at the age of sixteen. He spent the years from 1615 to 1624 preaching at various chapels and churches in the London area. Upon his appointment to the vicarage of St. Stephen's Parish in 1624, he became the spiritual leader of a large, wealthy, middle-class congregation. One of the members, Theophilus Eaton, a boyhood friend, remained his devoted friend and companion for years in the New World.

Davenport's solid reputation as a preacher had been built during the previous years, but his thinking now became more and more nonconformist. He inevitably came, as did Hooker, to the attention of Bishop Laud. By 1632 Davenport, definitely committed to the Puritan cause, became interested in the affairs of the Massachusetts Bay Company. He contributed fifty pounds to the corporation and also established friendly relations with John Cotton, a relationship which influenced him for many years. As Bishop Laud increased his efforts to achieve religious conformity among the clergy of the Church of England, Davenport's life and clerical duties became more precarious.

In 1633 when Laud became Archbishop of Canterbury, Davenport resigned his curacy and, as did many other clerics with strong Puritan inclinations, fled to Holland. He found the Netherlands not to his liking and after three years returned to England disguised as a country gentleman. Gathering together a group of his former parishioners, including Theophilus Eaton, who were willing to follow him to New England, he set sail for Boston aboard the *Hector* in April 1637. He was accompanied by his wife, Elizabeth, but his four-year-old son John had to be left behind. The child joined his parents two years later.

Arriving in Boston on June 26, 1637, Davenport found himself among old friends. John Cotton welcomed him and his wife, and insisted that they stay in his house for the nine months Davenport remained in the Boston area.

Davenport and his former parishioners arrived in Boston at a very critical time, when that colony was going through one of its troublesome domestic conflicts. They had no desire to become greatly involved in the religious controversies, nor did Davenport want to be in competition with the many other clergy of the Bay Colony. Eaton and others were merchants who had their minds set on a place for trade, and they could not find a harbor

John Davenport, the spiritual founder and leader of the New Haven Colony.

along the Massachusetts Bay coast not already overcrowded. The interior, such as the Connecticut River Valley, did not attract them. Davenport and Eaton strongly believed that God had other designs for them, which involved unoccupied territory.

The New Haven Colony

Hearing favorable reports about the region of the Quinnipiac River on Long Island Sound, Theophilus Eaton and some companions set out in August to explore the area. The attractive valley between the red hills and the calm, peaceful harbor delighted them. Eaton returned to Boston in the fall before the winter weather set in, but left seven of his companions at the site they had selected as their future home.

During the winter Eaton and Davenport made the final preparations for their company to join the seven in the early spring. On March 30, 1638, their group sailed from Boston for the Quinnipiac. The uncertain April weather made the journey a rough one as they sailed around Cape Cod and westward along the southern New England coast.

On the first Sunday after they arrived at New Haven, as they named the site, worship services were held under a large oak tree. John Davenport preached to the whole company, warning them of the temptations of the wilderness.

Soon afterward a "plantation covenant" was entered into, which carried a curious provision:

> As in matters that concern the gathering and ordering of a church, so also in all public affairs that concern civil order, they would all of them be ordered by the rules which the Scriptures held forth to them.

Thus began the "Bible State" of the New Haven Colony.

The Seven Pillars of New Haven

The land for the New Haven Colony was purchased from the local Indians. The Indians, who were to retain hunting and fishing rights, received "twelve coates of English trucking cloath, twelve alcumy spoones, twelve hatchetts, twelve hoes, two dozen of knives, twelve porengers & foure cases of French knives and sizers." The New Haven Colony, in general, treated the Indians much more fairly than other settlements did and, as a result, enjoyed friendly relations with them over the years.

The land was laid out in nine squares, the center one being set aside as a green, or marketplace. This central square is the now famous New Haven Green. The remaining eight squares and two adjoining "suburbs" were divided among the company.

The first settlers of New Haven were the most wealthy of any that emigrated to Connecticut from England. They erected within a few years large and handsome houses, similiar to the kind they had had at home. The Reverend John Davenport built his house in the form of a cross, and it had thirteen fireplaces. Theophilus Eaton built his in the form of an E, and it had nineteen fireplaces.

Davenport, Eaton, and their followers had their own ideas of what kind of government should be established in New Haven. They, like the settlers of Hartford, Wethersfield, and Windsor, had lived in the Bay Colony long enough to be familiar with the government there. However, their ideas of government differed even from those of the River Towns.

In June 1639 all the "freemen" of the New Haven Colony, about seventy in number, met in the large barn of Francis (or Robert) Newman and began the work of establishing "such civill order as might be most

This drawing of New Haven in 1641 shows the famous New Haven Green, which lies in the central square.

pleasing unto God, and for the choosing the fittest man for the foundation work of a church to be gathered." John Davenport raised some fundamental questions as to the qualifications of those who might be entrusted with the matters of government. He quoted to the assembled group from Proverbs 9:1: "Wisdom hath builded her house; she hath hewn out her seven pillars."

After hours of discussion and prayer those assembled decided:

45

> That church members onely shall be free burgesses, and thatt they onely shall chuse magistrates & officers among themselues to haue the power of transacting all the publique ciuill affayres of the Plantation[n], of makeing and repealing lawes, devideing of inheritances, decideing of differences thatt may arise and doeing all things or businesses of like nature.

The church would be organized by the selection of twelve men, who in turn would select seven from among themselves to serve as "the seven pillars." The leaders of the church and the colony would be largely the same. Thus was laid the foundation in New Haven of a theocracy, or a church state, in which a strictly limited church membership controlled the political government. Putting all the political power in the hands of the church denied to about half of the settlers of New Haven the right to vote for their rulers, since church membership was limited to those who professed to the rigid beliefs of the radical Puritan congregation.

Fortunately, seven pious, able, and prominent men were chosen as the first "seven pillars." They in turn selected nine others who met the religious qualifications. The sixteen then in October 1639 formed "a general court" of the town and elected a magistrate and four deputies.

Theophilus Eaton served as the magistrate for the first year and frequently afterward. He was responsible for the rejection of the jury trial in the colony because no mention could be found of it in the Bible, and the Scriptures were after all the source of all civil authority. Although Davenport was the pastor of the church, Eaton, headstrong and determined, remained in large part the dictator of the New Haven Colony until his death in 1658.

The New Frontiers

As early as 1639, a band of Puritans left New Haven and moved westward ten miles into the wilderness. They were the followers of the Reverend Peter Prudden. This was the third migration for the group in about as many years. They had left England in the company of John Davenport and Theophilus Eaton and in turn had followed them from Boston to New Haven.

The first migrants from the original Connecticut settlements left for basically the same reasons the original settlers left the Bay Colony. They were uncomfortable with the religious or political restraints set up by the local leaders, or they wanted more, or better, land than was available to them.

On the day the New Haven church was organized, August 22, 1639, Peter Prudden and his friends met separately and adopted their own church covenant. Soon after, Prudden's followers collected their families and their goods and left New Haven with their own loved pastor as their leader to found an independent community, the town of Milford, on the shores of Long Island Sound to the west of New Haven. Among the group were several former residents of Wethersfield, where Prudden had preached on a temporary basis the previous winter.

The role of a strong personality in the founding of new Connecticut towns should not be underestimated. Peter Prudden, an ideal pioneer leader, had a winning personality and sound common sense. This way of organizing new towns was characteristic of the Puritan method of settlement. The church, the government, and the land were all in the control of a single leader or group of leaders. In most instances, the church existed before the civil government was set up and sometimes even before the actual settlement began. Frequently isolated by geographic distance from the original settlements, the early settlers felt free to work out their religious, political, and economic destinies without interference from the outside, and the self-reliance of these groups typified the independent spirit that marked the early history of all Connecticut.

In general, the second-generation towns followed the method of land distribution used by the original settlements. This was based on the familiar common-law procedures of England. When a town was incorporated, all admitted "freemen"—that is, those who met the qualifications for voting in town elections—had a voice in the distribution of the land.

Milford, like other towns, worked out a system known as "sizing," whereby the amount of land granted to a family was made to compensate for the differences in quality or location. A local committee of "sizers" chose a piece of land representative of the general run of what was to be divided. This served as a "pattern." If the land in question did not fit the "pattern" in fertility and distance from the town common, the committee added additional land to the grant, and this additional land was free from taxes. If the land was more desirable than the pattern, they decreased the amount, and so on. Thus everyone was assured reasonably fair treatment.

Usually a portion of land in the center of the town was set aside as a common, for the use of everyone in the town. Here the church and/or the meetinghouse was erected, plus the local tavern and general store. Quite frequently the common was located at a crossroads or on either side of the main street. The social and religious life of the community required that everyone live within a short distance of the common, so that he could easily attend public worship and be subject to the influence of the town leaders.

The town leaders liked to keep their eyes on what everyone was doing. Thus they did not approve of people moving to the outlying sections of the town, where the clergy, the magistrates, and the self-righteous neighbors were not able to supervise their actions. Domestic privacy, as such, was all but unknown in seventeenth-century Connecticut. However, the movement toward unsettled areas continued, and in time, as permission was granted to build new meetinghouses and establish local governments, many of these outlying sections became new towns in their own right.

The town of Farmington lies to the west of Hartford, Wethersfield, and Windsor, and is separated from them by a small mountain range. Farmington, another of the second-generation towns, was settled in 1640 and incorporated in 1645. The original settlers of Farmington, former residents of Hartford, Wethersfield, and Windsor, exhibited the fundamental urge so characteristic of the evolving Yankees. This was the desire to possess more land of their own, for in the possession of land they saw their economic and political freedom established.

CHAPTER FOUR

From Puritan to Yankee

In July 1639 George Fenwick arrived by ship in New Haven with his wife, Lady Alice Fenwick, his son, Henry, and his sisters, Elizabeth and Mary. He was on his way to Fort Saybrook to become governor of the "River Connecticut," for John Winthrop, Jr.'s contract was terminating. Lion Gardiner's contract had also expired, and Gardiner anxiously wished to retire to his island off the coast of Long Island, now known as Gardiner's Island.

George Fenwick, one of the most prominent members of the Puritan party in England, visited the Saybrook Colony in 1636, but returned to England to arrange for the coming of his friends to the "city of refuge." He was the only one of the original Warwick grantees to come to Saybrook, and he served as governor of the colony until 1644.

Although deeply disappointed that his Puritan friends in England were never able or willing to leave, the Fenwicks nevertheless made the best of the situation and tried hard to transplant the life they had known in England to the shores of Long Island Sound. They built a "fair home" and planted apple and cherry trees around the house. Lady Alice, fond of flowers, had an herb garden, where she grew plants for medicinal purposes. As a manor lady she helped the people of the small settlement. She faced the lonely days with courage and tried to subdue her fear of the Indians, but the life of a colonist in the New World was not for Lady Alice, who longed for her friends and the familiar hedgerows of England.

The New England Confederation

In August 1639 a delegation from the General Court in Hartford approached Fenwick about the possibility of confederating the Connecticut colonies with the Massachusetts colonies. They found him cordial and willing to cooperate. However, during the early 1640's Saybrook continued its independent status. It grew very slowly and lost some of the military nature of its early days. In 1643 the Connecticut River towns asked Fenwick to join with them, and in September of that year he attended the first meeting of the New England Confederation in Boston.

After lengthy discussions the representatives of the Bay Colony, Plymouth, Connecticut, and New Haven proposed a union, the purpose of which was to "enter into a firm and perpetual league of friendship and amity." In order to provide for their common defense, each colony was expected to contribute funds in proportion to its adult male population. In addition two representatives were to attend an annual meeting where matters concerning Indian affairs, boundary disputes, fugitives from justice, and other common problems of the colonies would be decided.

In April 1644 Fenwick was elected to the General Court in Hartford as a magistrate (early Connecticut's term for a legislative representative) from Saybrook. The following December he sold the fort at Saybrook to the General Court of the colony of Connecticut. Included in the sale were all the buildings and equipment of the settlement and all lands including the western lands and rights claimed by his company under the Warwick Patent. Fenwick was to stay on and collect his price over a ten-year period from specified duties on all corn, "Biskett," livestock and furs transported downstream past the fort. Furthermore, he retained personal use of the house, the wharf, and the land adjoining the fort.

Following the death of his wife in childbirth in November 1645, a discouraged and homesick Fenwick returned to England, where he held important positions in Cromwell's government. Because of his busy career in England and unpleasant memories of Saybrook, he simply lost interest in Connecticut.

From December 1644 Saybrook was considered a Connecticut town, with all the normal responsibilities and privileges that entailed. The community grew rapidly and prospered thereafter, and so Connecticut gained strategic and practical control of the entire Connecticut River Valley.

The New England Confederation consisted of the Bay Colony, Plymouth, Connecticut, and New Haven. The confederation ensured that the colonies would protect each other from the Dutch and the Indians, and that they would work together to solve their other problems.

The New England Confederation functioned actively for two decades. Since six votes were needed to pass a resolution, the smaller colonies could prevent their complete domination by the larger and more populous colony of Massachusetts. Although the confederation proved ineffective in times of trouble, valuable lessons in intercolony cooperation were learned, and the confederation was largely responsible for saving New England from needless war with the Dutch and Indians.

The Code of 1650

The Fundamental Orders gave Connecticut its first constitution or written framework of government, but the Code of 1650 was its first organized code of laws. The Fundamental Orders provided the authority for the General Court to pass laws for the general well-being of the people, but it did not deal with the details—how the laws were to be carried out.

Law and authority are necessary to the survival of any society. The early settlers of Connecticut, speaking through their magistrates and the General Court, realized this. The English heritage of common law and statutes was not transported across the Atlantic with the Puritan emigrants in its entirety. The Law of Moses and the Bible influenced them quite as much.

As early as 1646 the General Court asked Roger Ludlow, author of the Fundamental Orders, to draw up a code of laws for the colony. Ludlow, a trained lawyer and one of the few in the colony, adapted both the Massachusetts Bay Laws and Liberties of 1647 and the English common law to the needs of Connecticut. He abolished many out-of-date technicalities from the common law, such as primogeniture (which passed the bulk of a dead man's estate entirely to his first-born son, leaving little or nothing for his other offspring) and the practice of arbitrarily imprisoning men for debt.

The importance of civil liberties and the equal protection of the law were emphasized in the preamble to Ludlow's code:

> That no mans life bee taken away, no mans honor or good name shall bee stained, no mans person shall be arrested, restrained, banished, dismembered nor any way punnished; no man shall bee deprived of his wife or children, no mans goods or estate shall bee taken away from him, nor any wayes indamaged, vnder colour of Law or countenance of Authority, vnless it bee by the vertue or equity of some express Law of the Country warranting the same, established by a Generall Courte, and sufficiently published, or in case of the defect of a Law in any perticular case, by the word of God.

Thus, long before Thomas Jefferson and the Declaration of Independence, Connecticut's code of laws concerned itself with the rule of law and the protection of individual rights.

The provisions of Mr. Ludlow's Code, as it was commonly known, reflected many of the pressing problems of the times, from the defense of the colony to the operation of "an Ordinary" or inn. The sections dealing with the care and upbringing of children clearly stated the responsibilities and obligations of both the adults and the children. The legal age was twenty-one, the age of understanding was sixteen, and the age of knowing right from wrong—particularly in cases of lying—was fourteen. There was very little involving the lives and morality of the people that was not covered in one of the sections of the code.

Its seventy-eight sections were arranged alphabetically, and each section spelled out the duties and responsibilities of citizenship or the nature of a crime and its particular punishment. Therefore, each settler in Connecticut knew in advance what his duties were and the risk he took when he broke the law. The code did much to provide stability for the Puritan way of life. Many of the punishments may seem harsh to the modern reader. For example, the use of profanity was punishable by a fine or a period of one to three hours in the stocks, and drinking in the inn after nine o'clock brought the same punishment. Anyone who challenged or interrupted the preacher would be censured the first time, and if it happened again, he would be fined five pounds or would be placed on a stool four feet high on lecture day, "with a paper fixed on his breast written with Capital Letters, AN OPEN AND OBSTINATE CONTEMNER OF GODS HOLY ORDINANCES." These practices of Connecticut's Puritans did not, however, differ from those generally accepted in Old England at that time.

The Puritan Family

Comparatively few newcomers migrated to Connecticut after the first rush of settlers in the 1630's and 1640's. Conditions in England changed, and the Puritans came to power in 1649 with the death of Charles I. Men still refugeed from England for political and religious reasons, but those fleeing from the excesses of the Puritan government naturally did not come to Puritan New England.

In spite of the decline in migration, New England's population increased steadily as a result of the natural high birthrate. Within a decade or two of the original settlements the Three River Towns were sending forth individuals and families to make new settlements elsewhere in Connecticut.

Throughout this process the family remained the basic social and religious unit. The Puritan family was a model of piety and filial respect. The authority of the father over his wife and children was usually absolute, and behind the figure of the father stood the awesome presence of the magistrates and the clergy.

When a woman married, she gave up everything to her husband. She came under his complete authority and devoted herself exclusively to the

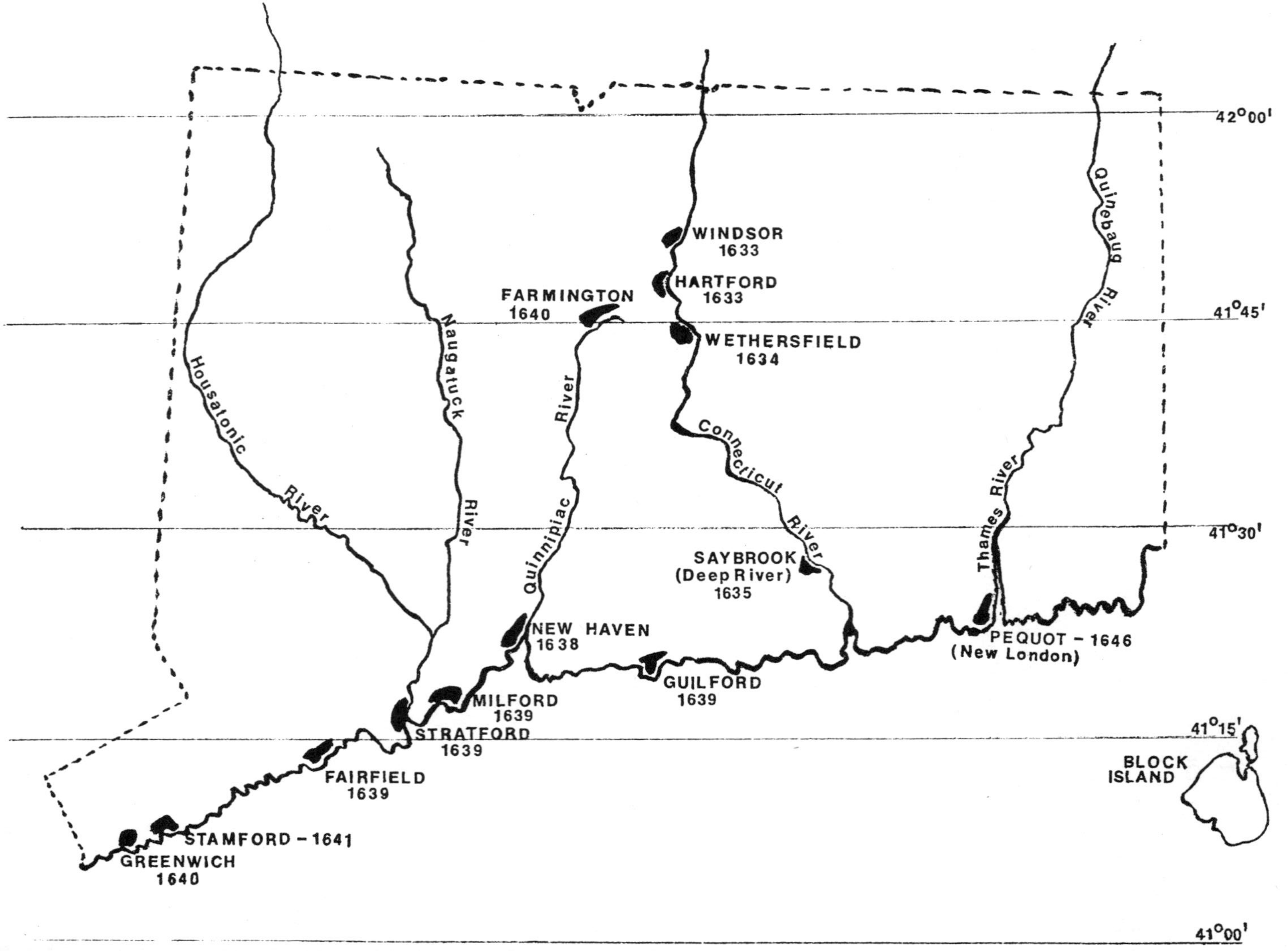
42°00'
41°45'
41°30'
41°15'
41°00'
WINDSOR
1633
HARTFORD
1633
WETHERSFIELD
1634
FARMINGTON
1640
Housatonic River
Naugatuck River
Quinnipiac River
Connecticut River
Thames River
Quinebaug River
SAYBROOK
(Deep River)
1635
NEW HAVEN
1638
GUILFORD
1639
MILFORD
1639
STRATFORD
1639
FAIRFIELD
1639
STAMFORD - 1641
GREENWICH
1640
PEQUOT - 1646
(New London)
BLOCK
ISLAND

management of his household. Her place was "to guid the house & not guid the Husband."

Family discipline was rigid, and the father was held personally responsible for the behavior of all members of his household. Therefore all signs of disobedience or delinquency were nipped in the bud. No father wanted to be punished for the misdeeds of his sons.

The father's first duty to his children was to give them food, shelter, and protection. Then according to the law, every father was to see to it that his children were instructed "in some honest lawful calling, labour or imployment, either in husbandry [farming], or some other trade profitable for themselves. . . ." Every child was put to some kind of useful work before he or she reached the age of seven.

Girls could only follow the career of housewife and mother. Boys, however, had some measure of choice and usually decided on their life's occupation between ten and fourteen. In large families, where children had varying talents, probably only one son followed in his father's trade, and the others took up different occupations. Since training in almost every craft was gained through a seven-year apprenticeship to a master, most boys chose what they wanted to do in life at an early age.

Large families were the rule, and several generations usually lived under the same roof. Girls married at sixteen and seventeen and had six or seven children in rapid succession; frequently they died in childbirth or of disease. Second wives usually had fewer children and an easier time, for there were older children to help with the household chores.

The life of children was not easy. They were treated like little men or women and dressed in the same clothing styles as their parents. At the table they were not to speak unless spoken to and were expected to eat without question whatever was given to them.

Because medical knowledge was limited, contagious diseases spread unchecked. Many did live to a ripe old age, but life expectancy at birth was relatively short. If infants survived the rigors of birth, they might die a few months later of severe colds, sore throats, smallpox, diphtheria, measles, or any of innumerable common diseases.

Servants were considered members of the household and directly re-

Ten more towns were settled within thirteen years of the founding of the Three River Towns.

sponsible to the father as head of the household. In the seventeenth century, anyone who worked for another in whatever capacity was called a servant, whether he served in a voluntary or involuntary capacity. Voluntary servants might be hired, apprenticed, or indentured for a limited period of time, usually seven years. Involuntary servants were either Indian or black slaves, but slaves never were held in any significant number in Connecticut.

The Meetinghouse

The meetinghouse became the center and symbol of the community in early Connecticut towns. It was built either on or closely adjacent to the town common, and was the most centrally located building of the community. The rich and the influential town leaders built their homes near it, and it served not only as a place of worship, but also as a town hall and public storehouse for the town's armies. Nearby were the other public buildings and facilities: the schoolhouse, the blacksmith shop, the general store, the ordinary or inn, the jail, the whipping post, and the pillory.

The early meetinghouses were built simply, as were most of the other

The first meetinghouse in Connecticut was built in 1635 in Hartford. The Reverend Thomas Hooker preached here.

buildings in town. The earliest ones, built of rough-cut lumber, were usually square. The roof was pyramidal and terminated in a central watchtower, which later became a belfry. (It was the middle of the eighteenth century before bells came into general use.) The meetinghouses were not large, only forty or fifty feet square, but they could hold the entire population of the early towns.

The Sabbath, or the Lord's Day, began at sunset on Saturday. At that time all unnecessary work ceased, and until sunset of the following day, strict religious observances filled the waking hours. Attending the Sabbath services was a serious matter, and on Sunday everyone, unless sick or disabled, gathered at the meetinghouse at the beating of a drum or the sound of a horn. Since there was no Sunday school, children attended the regular services.

Social rank determined the seating in the meetinghouse. The elders and deacons sat closest to the pulpit in the front, and the rest of the congregation filled the pews behind them, usually the men on one side and the women on the other. Children and servants sat in the back seats or in the gallery. At first rough benches were used, but later square pews were introduced and assigned. Thus each household and every person had an assigned place in meeting, and they were expected to be there when the service began.

The Puritan sermons were long—two or three hours, sometimes five—and the prayers often could be an hour long. Strict discipline was observed, and any tendency to fall asleep was promptly checked by using "long staves tipped with brass" to rap "unmercifully the heads of slumbering or disorderly men or boys" while the faces of the women and girls were brushed "with a hare's foot appended to the rod."

Since there were few hymnals, a deacon would read a line of a psalm at a time and then the congregation would sing it. It occasionally took a half hour or more to sing one of the psalms.

In the early days the meetinghouse was not heated. In the cold weather the ministers often preached in their overcoats, with a muffler about the neck and mittens upon their hands. In the coldest weather the women carried heated stones or little hand stoves in their muffs, while the men often pulled bags over their feet to keep warm. The sermons frequently dealt with the struggle between good and evil, and the ministers spent a great deal of time describing the fiery depths of hell. Though this may have warmed the inner conscience of the Puritans, it did little to warm their outer bodies.

The ministers wielded great power and authority from their pulpits. The people looked up to them, and laws were made and public policy formulated in accordance with their views. They were, without exception, leaders in every way among the people, men of birth, breeding, and education.

Education

These ministers, graduates of the great universities of Oxford and Cambridge in England, naturally desired to start schools and colleges in New England. But most of the common people, too—even those with so little education that they could not write their names—wanted their children to read and write, so that they might read the Bible and the laws of the colony and take part in the government.

Among the early Puritans education was a means of ensuring the religious welfare of their children. The main business of education in their minds was to prepare the children for salvation, since all children were thought to be born evil as well as ignorant. They were considered half saved by their parents' conversion to the Puritan faith, but it was only through education that they could be wholly saved. Therefore, the Code of 1650 made the Puritan father responsible for seeing that his children could "read the Inglish tounge" and the "Capitall lawes" and at least once a week he was to hear his children's catechism.

In 1639 in Hartford, the Reverend John Higginson established Connecticuts' first school. In New Haven on Christmas Day 1641, it was voted "thatt a free schoole be set up in this towne"; the teacher, Ezekial Cheever, was to teach the classics and English as well as arithmetic and Latin.

Other settlements established similar schools, built schoolhouses within a year or two of the towns' founding, and paid teachers out of public funds. The Code of 1650, established by the General Court, ordered that every township of fifty families "shall then forthwith appoint one within theire Towne to teach all such children as resorte to him, to write and read, whose wages shall bee paid either by the parents or masters of such children." When the towns grew to one hundred families, a grammar school

The horn book was used by children to learn the alphabet and the Lord's Prayer; compare its size to a man's ring.

was to be set up so as to prepare the youths for the university. The only college in New England was Harvard College, founded in 1636 at Cambridge, Massachusetts.

Thus compulsory education, a fundamental concept in today's world, was put into practice during the first decades of Connecticut's history. It was then a revolutionary notion, unknown throughout most of Europe.

His Brother's Keeper

The passion among the Puritans for running other people's lives received a free rein in early Connecticut, and observant neighbors always deemed it their duty to report violations of the social and religious codes. This came under the heading of "doing the Lord's work." Every Puritan believed that he was commissioned by God to be his brother's keeper.

Since the family unit held such a strong position in early Connecticut, young unmarried men and women were not permitted to live alone or in pairs. The town fathers usually assigned them to live with families. In 1652 the town of Windsor did allow an exception when it permitted two young men to keep house together, provided they lived soberly and did not "entertain idle persons to the evil expense of time by day or night." Wives whose husbands were away could not entertain even overnight guests or lodgers because they might give the "appearance of sin."

The early rulers of Connecticut were very much concerned with sin. There was no end to the ways in which a Puritan could sin. Some of the most common ways of sinning were swearing, Sabbath-breaking, sleeping during sermons, drinking in taverns, overdressing, and sexual laxity.

Both in the Connecticut colony and in the New Haven colony adultery was a sin and a capital offense. The punishment for it was, in today's terms, "cruel and unusual." Fines, brandings, whippings, and the wearing of the letter "A" sewed to the clothing were the most common forms of

The pillory, employed in both the American colonies and Europe, was used in punishing those who committed the less serious crimes.

punishment, for punishment was aimed not so much at improving the sinner as at demonstrating to God that the town fathers did not condone sin.

Divorce, like marriage, came under the jurisdiction of the civil authorities and could be granted for "adultery, fraudulent contract, or willful desertion for three years with totall neglect of duty, or seven years providentiall absence being not heard of after due enquiry made and certifyed." Three divorces are known to have been granted to wives in early years, for willful desertion and nonsupport by their husbands. But such cases were rare.

Thus no part of the domestic life of the Puritan family was excluded from the authority of the church and the state, or the keen eyes of ever-watchful neighbors.

The Emerging Yankee

The popular version of the Puritans as a joyless and hopeless people has some basis in fact—strict discipline in social and public affairs was enforced in Connecticut communities. Yet social life was marked by many festive days: training days for the militia, election days, town meeting days, weddings. Even funerals became occasions for general community gatherings to make merry, gossip, and eat.

The children who grew to maturity after the settling of Connecticut had no memories of life in Old England. The persecutions of the Puritan Revolution had only a historical meaning to them. As the lives of the residents were conditioned and shaped by the events and environment of New England, a new and different kind of personality soon developed.

In the last half of the seventeenth century, Connecticut, because of its geographic location, became one of the most insular and decentralized of the American colonies. The people in the several towns lived placid and peaceful lives and willingly submitted to the rule of their preachers and magistrates. They rarely allowed unsettling ideas to disturb their close-knit society.

Connecticut came to be known as the Land of Steady Habits—orthodox religion and traditional ways. Furthermore, conformity became one of the most distinguishing features and characteristics of the emerging Connecticut Yankee.

CHAPTER FIVE

The Royal Colony

Puritan rule in England ended in 1660, when Charles II was officially restored to the throne. The sense of security that had existed in New England during the rule of Oliver Cromwell and the Puritans was shattered, for Connecticut's leaders realized that they were now operating their government without any firm legal basis. The Warwick Patent, the Fundamental Orders, and the various Indian grants had no official backing in the eyes of the restored monarchy. Moreover, the new government in England, unfriendly to Puritans and their way of life, could and possibly would assume complete control over all the New England colonies.

During the years of the Commonwealth little official attention had been paid to New England and especially Connecticut. Now Connecticut's leaders feared that the restored king might give the control of Connecticut to the more powerful colony of Massachusetts. So on March 14, 1661, the General Court voted its allegiance to the new king but also voted to petition for a charter.

Because both Massachusetts and the Dutch had strong desires to control Connecticut and because its boundaries were largely undefined, Connecticut felt that it needed a charter. The charter petition pointed out that part of the land in Connecticut had been purchased from the Indians and from George Fenwick and the rest had been acquired by conquest. It also emphasized that considerable hard labor, sacrifice, and expense had gone into the improvement of the land. In order to make things easier for the

British monarch, the Connecticut leaders sent Governor John Winthrop, Jr., to England with a draft copy of a charter for the king's signature.

John Winthrop, Jr.

Governor John Winthrop, Jr., a man of many talents, was at various times a scholar, an inventor, a statesman, and a physician. Born in Groton, England, on February 12, 1605, he was the eldest son of the future governor of Massachusetts. He studied medicine at Dublin University and law in London for a short time. In 1631 he followed his father to America, where he became involved in various industrial enterprises, especially iron manufacturing, and for years he also practiced medicine.

Winthrop had been actively involved in the 1635 attempted settlement at Saybrook, as we have seen. He returned to Connecticut in 1646 and founded Pequot, or New London, at the mouth of the Thames River, ten miles or so east of the Connecticut. His land claim in this region was based on promises made to him by the former proprietors of the Warwick Patent, who had backed the earlier Saybrook venture. In the process of making this settlement, Winthrop acquired title to 10,000 to 12,000 acres of land east and northeast of New London.

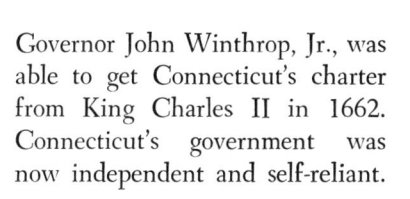

Governor John Winthrop, Jr., was able to get Connecticut's charter from King Charles II in 1662. Connecticut's government was now independent and self-reliant.

He became a magistrate of the colony of Connecticut in 1651 and was elected governor six years later. His popularity with the people was so great that the General Court voted in 1660 to eliminate the provision of the Fundamental Orders limiting a governor's tenure in office to only one year in any two. As a result Winthrop was able to serve as governor until his death in 1676.

Winthrop's greatest service to Connecticut was obtaining the colony's charter from Charles II. His experience, knowledge, and personality made him the ideal choice for achieving this goal, and besides he had influential and powerful friends at court in England. During the many months of his stay in England, he used his time to good advantage socially as well as officially, for he was admitted to membership in the newly founded Royal Society—an honor that was to be accorded to very few Americans.

The Charter of 1662

After months of negotiation Charles II finally signed the charter, whose provisions were based on the draft prepared by Winthrop, and the privy seal was affixed. The writ of privy seal was secured on April 23, 1662, and that is considered the formal date of Connecticut's charter.

Winthrop was not able to leave England immediately, so the charter was entrusted to two Massachusetts men, and after their arrival in Boston, they presented it, on September 3, to Samuel Wyllys and John Talcott, who were in Boston as delegates to the New England Confederation. Wyllys and Talcott brought the document to Hartford.

The Charter of 1662, a remarkable document, gave the people of Connecticut not only a clear legal basis for their colony but also a high degree of self-government. It defined the boundaries of the colony as Narragansett Bay on the east, the Massachusetts line on the north, and Long Island Sound on the south. On the west, Connecticut was to extend all the way to the "South Sea," or the Pacific Ocean. The boundary lines were so vaguely generous that they were later to provoke disputes with Rhode Island, Massachusetts, New York, and Pennsylvania.

The charter established Connecticut as a corporation with John Winthrop, Jr., and others as a corporate body called the "Governour and Company of the English Colony of Connecticut in New England in

America." The freemen of the colony were to enjoy all the "liberties and Immunities" of natural-born Englishmen provided they took the oath of supremacy to the Crown. Full judicial powers were granted to the legislature or to the governor or deputy and any six assistants. The law-making powers resided in the legislature, but that body could not enact any laws "contrary to the lawes and Statutes of this our Realme of England." In other words, the charter gave full executive, legislative, and judicial authority to the Connecticut colony, and the king did not even reserve the right to review the laws of the colony.

A further provision granted the freemen of Connecticut land tenure similar to that of the Manor of East Greenwich, which was then the freest of any in England, and in return the Crown was to receive one fifth of all gold and silver mined in Connecticut. Although Connecticut failed to obtain exemption from English custom duties, it received many other favorable provisions. So Connecticut was independent in all ways except for its allegiance to the Crown.

The Charter of 1662 to all intents and purposes did away with New Haven as a separate colony, and on December 13, 1664, the New Haven colony voted to become officially a part of Connecticut.

The Regicides

When word of Charles's restoration to the throne reached New Haven, the announcement caused a great deal of excitement in that Puritan stronghold. It was known that two of the judges who had signed the death warrant of Charles I in 1649 were staying at the home of the Reverend John Davenport.

At his restoration, Charles II pardoned all who had fought against the Crown in the Puritan Revolution, except the fifty-nine judges who had signed his father's death warrant. These judges were known as the regicides, or king killers. Of the fifty-nine judges, twenty-four had died, ten were executed, and nineteen imprisoned for life. The remaining six had fled the country.

Two of those who had fled were William Goffe and Edward Whalley. They crossed the Atlantic to Boston, but they felt their lives were in danger there, too, so they traveled on to New Haven. Sure enough, they had scarcely left Boston when an order arrived for their arrest.

The authorities in Massachusetts, Connecticut, and New Haven were in a quandary. They wanted to protect the regicides, but they did not want to incur the king's wrath, as they would certainly do if they openly disobeyed his order. Calling meetings, they discussed the matter and decided to use delaying tactics, to allow Goffe and Whalley time to escape from the two zealous young agents who had been authorized to track them down.

As the royal agents approached New Haven, the Reverend John Davenport preached a sermon from Isaiah 16:3–4: "Hide the outcasts; bewray not him that wandereth. Let mine outcasts dwell with thee, Moab; be thou a covert to them from the face of the spoiler." As the people listened, they understood the sermon without any need of personal application.

Eventually Goffe and Whalley hid in a cave on top of West Rock in New Haven, later called Judges' Cave, and spent the summer there being fed by friends and sympathizers. When they felt that their presence in the New Haven area was endangering their friends, Goffe and Whalley traveled north to Hadley, Massachusetts, then a remote frontier town. There they lived out the rest of their lives hidden in the home of the Reverend John Russell.

A third regicide, John Dixwell, came to New Haven soon after Goffe and Whalley moved to Hadley. He assumed the name of James David and lived happily with his wife and children until his death in 1689. Only after his death did his true identity become known.

The episode of the regicides shows that the sympathies of the people were with the Puritan cause even though they understood the advantages of cooperating with the new royal monarch.

King Philip's War

For more than thirty years the white settlers lived in peace and harmony with their Indian neighbors. During those years the Indians grew familiar with the white man's ways and in many instances became part of his communities and dependent upon him. The missionary work of the Reverend John Eliot among the Indians was copied by a few preachers

King Philip, also known as Metacomet, was successful in fighting the white man for one year, until the spring of 1676. By the summer his uprising had failed and in August he was shot by one of his own Indians.

in Connecticut, but of the four thousand or more Indians in New England who became Christians, only a few lived in Connecticut.

Early in the spring of 1675, a Christianized Indian was murdered near Plymouth, Massachusetts. The conviction and hanging of three Indians for this murder sparked a local conflict between Plymouth and the chief of the Wampanoags, King Philip.

Philip was the second son of Massasoit, the great friend of the first settlers of Plymouth. Over the years, as he saw the hunting grounds of his tribe being taken over by the white settlers, he grew resentful and bitter toward the whites. After his father's death in 1661, his older brother Alexander became the chief. Alexander shared Philip's fears and frustrations, and because he was accused of plotting against the Plymouth settlers, he was called before the town council. Alexander proclaimed his innocence, but shortly afterward he became sick and died.

Philip believed his brother had been poisoned by the white men. For several years he nursed fancied wrongs. Hatred and the spirit of revenge grew within him as he looked about and saw his tribe, once masters over many miles of land, now crowded into the small peninsula of Mount Hope on Narragansett Bay. He visited the scattered tribes of New England and played upon their fears and suspicions of the white man. A secret council of war was then called. Philip recalled to the chiefs of the neighboring tribes their past glories and pointed out the prospects of their having to be tamely submissive to the whites in the future. Finally, after much discussion and argument, they agreed to his plan of driving the white man out of Massachusetts and all New England.

The first Indian attacks against the white settlers were in the Plymouth, Massachusetts Bay, and Rhode Island areas. The Indians, perhaps remembering the destruction of the Pequots, did not attack in Connecticut. However, all of the New England colonies sent troops to the aid of the settlers in Massachusetts. Connecticut sent over 300 soldiers plus 150 Pequot and Mohegan Indian allies. Uncas, the aged leader of the Mohegans, was anxious for the opportunity to strike at his old enemies, the Narragansetts, who had joined forces with Philip.

During the summer of 1675, the fighting spread from eastern to central Massachusetts and to the upper Connecticut River Valley. Connecticut's northern frontier became exposed. By late summer rumors grew that there was unrest among the Connecticut Valley Indians.

At summer's end, it appeared that the Indians had the upper hand. Fear and despair spread throughout Connecticut. The colony's leaders took steps to prevent the war from spreading southward. Night watches were established in all towns in the northern part of the colony, and armed patrols guarded the workers in the fields and along the roads. Additional troops were called up.

In December about a thousand men from Connecticut and Massachusetts engaged the Indians in a great battle in a swamp near South Kingston, Rhode Island. The Indians were severely weakened, and peace negotiations opened, but neither side fully trusted the other. As a result, both Indians and whites made preparations for spring campaigns.

With the coming of spring in 1676, Philip appeared in the Farmington River Valley with a band of warriors and burned homes in Granby and Simsbury. Fortunately no white settlers were killed, for they had already fled across the mountain to Windsor for safety.

The almost unchecked series of Indian victories came to an end in April, and by summer the white settlers, making use of their Pequot and Mohegan allies, brought the war to a close. Philip's wife and son were captured and sold as slaves in Bermuda. However, Philip himself continued to elude the white troops and returned to Mount Hope, where he was finally shot by one of his own Indians. His head was cut off, carried to Plymouth, and placed on a pole as a warning to all other Indians of the vengeance of the colonists.

King Philip's War lasted only a little over a year, and yet the Indians had been a far more dangerous enemy in the 1670's than in the Pequot War. Their weapons were no longer just the arrow, the tomahawk, the spear, and the scalping knife. They had acquired firearms with powder and shot and learned the most vulnerable points of attack. In all of New England more than a thousand people were killed, hundreds of homes were set on fire, and numerous villages destroyed. As in the Pequot War, the Indians used surprise and ambush as their main methods of fighting, but the colonists used troops of infantry and cavalry under officers experienced with the ways of the Indians, and their revenge on Indian men, women, and children was swift and murderous.

To the Puritans of 1675–76, Philip symbolized the devil himself, but the brave warrior king has won a place for himself in history as the first of many American Indian leaders who tried unsuccessfully to defend their lands against white invaders. To this day, descendants of his enemies, occupying his old homeland, are open admirers of Philip's courage and dignity.

Andros and the Charter

King Philip's War posed a physical threat to the settlers of Connecticut, but an even greater political threat occurred in 1674, when Charles II granted a new charter for New York to his brother James, the Duke of York. This new charter gave the duke "all the Land from the west side of Connecticut River, to the East side of Delaware Bay." Charles seemed to have little knowledge of the geography of the New World. This one lighthearted grant of distant lands was to cause decades of trouble to the future states of Maryland, Delaware, Pennsylvania, New Jersey, and

Sir Edmund Andros, a vain and proud man, had very few friends in New England. After his arrest in Boston, he was tried in England and immediately released. Later he served as governor of Virginia (1692–1698) and Maryland (1693–1694).

Connecticut, for it cut ruthlessly across the boundaries of numerous other grants and patents.

James appointed Major Edmund Andros as Governor of New York and sent him to demand that western Connecticut be turned over to New York. This came as a shock to the Connecticut General Court, which reminded Andros of Connecticut's rights under its Charter of 1662. Nevertheless, on July 8, 1675, Major Andros appeared off Saybrook with several ships and demanded the surrender of the fort. But the flag of England flew over the fort, and the Connecticut militia manning it had orders from the General Court to resist its surrender. So Andros had second thoughts. He decided not to press his demand and withdrew to New York.

Governor Winthrop and Major Andros eventually worked out a compromise. Many of the towns on Long Island had been founded by settlers from the New Haven colony, so Connecticut had claimed jurisdiction there. Now it gave up these claims, and in return New York agreed to surrender its claims to western Connecticut.

When Charles died in 1685, he was succeeded by his brother James. During the first year of his reign, James II revoked the charters granted to

Massachusetts and Rhode Island and demanded the Connecticut charter. He planned to organize New England under one government, and in June 1686 Edmund Andros was appointed to the governorship of the Dominion of New England. This move was intended to destroy the Puritan political domination over the New England colonies. James, a fervent Catholic, could not forget the "murder" of his father by the Puritan regicides.

Andros ordered Connecticut to surrender its charter and become annexed to Massachusetts. From Hartford Governor Robert Treat sent him an answer that Andros interpreted to mean that Connecticut would comply. On the afternoon of October 31, 1687, he arrived in Hartford, attended by a bodyguard of seventy-five men, to obtain the charter and assume authority over the colony.

The Charter Oak Tradition

What happened during the next several hours has become one of Connecticut's most cherished traditions.

Andros met with Governor Treat and members of the General Court. The king's commission, appointing him governor of all New England, was read, and then by virtue of this authority, Andros demanded the formal surrender of the Charter of 1662. Governor Treat pleaded long and eloquently for the liberties of the people of Connecticut, and other officials followed him with passionate speeches on the danger and discomforts men of Connecticut had experienced in establishing and expanding their colony. A reply was made by Andros, and by the time he finished, the afternoon was spent and darkness closing in. The charter was finally brought out and unrolled on the table around which the officials were seated, while the room filled up with people and outside the building farmers and townsmen gathered to learn what would happen.

As the darkness increased, candles were lighted. Then Andrew Leete, a man in poor health but a member of the General Court, arose and leaned on the table. "That Charter is in force at this hour," he said slowly. "No judgment has been rendered against it. It was granted under the Great Seal of England and cannot be surrendered unless the surrender is given under the seal of this Colony. Remember Charles I's last words—'that measures obtained by force do not endure.'" As he uttered those words, Leete fell unconscious across the table and knocked over the candles.

The famed Charter Oak, which hid the Charter of 1662 for one year, succumbed to old age and high winds in 1856.

The room was immediately plunged into darkness. The candles were relighted as quickly as flint and tinder would permit. In the confusion and darkness, however, someone had taken the charter from the table.

In the darkness, tradition says, Nathaniel Stanley handed the charter through an open window to Captain Joseph Wadsworth of Hartford, who then carried the charter to an old oak tree. There he wrapped the charter in his tunic and hid it in a hollow portion of what came to be known as the Charter Oak.

This tree had been preserved by the early settlers at the request of the Indians who said, "It has been the guide of our ancestors for centuries as to the time of planting our corn. When the leaves are the size of a mouse's ears, then is the time to put it in the ground." The Charter Oak remained standing until it was blown down during a severe gale in August 1856.

When Andros realized that he had been tricked and that there was nothing he could do about it, he announced the end of the government of Connecticut under the royal charter.

For the next year Governor Andros ruled New England with a strictness that pleased no one. He restricted the freedoms of the people. He required a payment of money for all marriages that were to be performed, and he established other fees. He taxed the people heavily and required widows and children to come to Boston to settle estates. The rule of Andros in New England was as despotic and arbitary as was the rule of James II in old England.

Connecticut, however, did not suffer as heavily as Massachusetts, because former Governor Treat was appointed a member of Andros' council, and he was able to modify many of the harsh orders concerning Connecticut.

In 1688 the Glorious Revolution toppled the Catholic James II from the throne. The predominately Protestant Parliament led the revolt and invited William of Orange and his wife Mary, both Protestants, to assume the throne with limited powers. Mary was James's daughter by his first wife. A Bill of Rights was passed in 1689, as were other safeguards of liberty.

When the news of the revolution reached Boston, Andros was arrested and put in prison. In Connecticut the charter was brought out of its hiding place, and Robert Treat was again chosen as governor. The General Court pledged its loyalty to the new monarchs and wrote that they had never surrendered the charter given by Charles II. The old laws were once more declared to be in force, and in Connecticut it was pretty much business as usual.

CHAPTER SIX

The Land of Steady Habits

The Puritan who settled Connecticut believed that he was "God's chosen custodian of religious truth and morality." His grandchildren, however, looked at the world differently. They were influenced as much by their environment as he had been by his. The changing conditions of their world and their increased comforts brought the "golden age of piety" in Connecticut to a close by the last quarter of the seventeenth century.

There were various causes that contributed to the decline in Puritan piety and in church attendance. Life in the wilderness had an "indianizing" effect on the settlers and their offspring. The Reverend John Davenport had sensed this danger when he preached his first sermon in New Haven on "the temptations in the wilderness." Furthermore, the disasters, the horrors, and the fears that accompanied the Indian wars, the political changes in England, and the Andros rule in New England altered social conditions and took men's minds from spiritual things. The influx of new settlers was also a factor.

As the end of the seventeenth century approached, population patterns changed dramatically throughout Connecticut. The land which had first been put under cultivation began to wear out, and the search was on for new homes and farm lands on both sides of the Connecticut River valley. Before 1690, Connecticut had only thirty towns. In the thirty years after that date twenty new ones were settled.

As a flood of migrants pushed westward from southeastern Massachusetts, eastern Connecticut began to fill up, two or three decades before western Connecticut. From 1670 to 1700 Connecticut's population increased from about 12,000 to over 30,000. Large families were common, and eight to twenty children in a family were not unusual. By 1730 the population had again doubled.

The Half-Way Covenant, which was debated hotly in the 1660's, permitted persons who had been baptized but not converted to acquire formal church membership. They had only to make a public profession of the Puritan faith. The covenant eventually won widespread but not universal acceptance. Before the end of the century, deep differences of opinion began to appear, especially between the older church members and the younger, and these caused much hard feelings.

Despite great efforts to maintain religious uniformity, a few religious dissenters, such as Quakers, Anglicans, and Baptists, entered the colony. The Puritans viewed them, especially the Quakers, as a menace to the social order and fined them for absenting themselves from church. In 1675 Connecticut relaxed the laws against the Quakers, but this was done chiefly to remain in the good graces of the Quaker colony of Rhode Island, for King Philip's War was just beginning. Later, when the activities of the Anglicans and the Baptists began to worry the Congregational churches— as the Puritan churches were then being called—there was a revival of the persecuting spirit against those of different religious beliefs.

In 1708 the Saybrook Platform was drawn up by a group of ministers and members of congregations in the hopes that it would secure order and uniformity among the Congregationalists. The platform was ordered printed and distributed at the expense of the colony and was the first book printed in Connecticut. The Saybrook Platform did much to bring temporary religious peace to Connecticut.

Gurdon Saltonstall

The Saybrook Platform had the approval of Governor Gurdon Saltonstall, an influential minister. Saltonstall was the first clergyman in Connecticut to take the oath of governor.

Saltonstall was born in 1666 in Haverhill, Massachusetts. At fourteen he entered Harvard College and was graduated in 1684. After studying for a few years with local clergymen, he accepted the invitation of the

The Reverend Gurdon Saltonstall was the first clergyman elected governor of the colony. He gained office after Governor Fitz-John Winthrop's death, and served from 1707 to 1724.

First Church of Christ in New London to be its minister. He was ordained with great ceremony on November 19, 1691.

As a result of his scholarly sermons, his general knowledge of many things, and his dependable judgment, he soon became a figure of importance in the community. In fact, the town gave him an appropriation of money to erect a home "suitable to his dignity."

Marriage had not been considered a sacrament by the Puritans, and until 1686 all marriages were performed by the magistrates. After that date the clergy were also empowered to perform the marriage ceremony. Occasionally, however, a man and woman insisted on living together out of wedlock. According to an old New London tradition, the Reverend Mr. Saltonstall confronted such a couple one day and said to them, "Do you really, John, take this your servant-maid, bought with your money, for your wife? Do you, Mary, take this man so much older than yourself for your husband?" When he received an affirmative answer from both, he exclaimed, "Then I pronounce you, according to the laws of the colony, man and wife." Ususally, however, it was necessary to announce ahead of time the intention to wed, and no ceremony could take place until eight days after the announcement of "a contract of espousals."

Fitz-John Winthrop, the son of John Winthrop, Jr., was a member of Saltonstall's congregation and as governor sought his advice on many matters. Consequently, Saltonstall's fame spread throughout the colony. When Winthrop died in 1707, the General Assembly, recognizing Saltonstall's ability and knowledge of the affairs of the colony, appointed him governor. Because there was some oppostion to a clergyman being governor, Saltonstall resigned his parish. The voters confirmed his appointment in May 1708, and he was reelected annually until his death in 1724.

The Collegiate School Becomes Yale

One of the dreams of the Reverend John Davenport was of founding a college in the New Haven colony, for "the better training up of youth, that, through God's blessing, they may be fitted for public service hereafter either in church or commonwealth." During Davenport's lifetime, New Haven was not large enough to support a college, but many others shared his dream, and in 1701 the General Assembly received a petition from a group of clergymen to establish a college in the colony, to avoid "the distance and expense of sending boys to Harvard."

New Haven was a logical site. Although its population at the end of the seventeenth century was only around a thousand, it boasted one out of every thirty Harvard College graduates.

So a charter was given "to erect a Collegiate School," and ten clergymen were appointed "Trustees, Partners, or Undertakers for the said School." They represented the most prominent towns and were quite evenly distributed among the different parts of the colony. Before the year was over, they met at Saybrook and drew up the rules to govern the school. Since they were all Harvard graduates, they "wished to make this college for Connecticut what their *alma mater* had been for Massachusetts."

The early years of the Collegiate School were not very auspicious. The school's student body was very small and its resources very limited. A controversy developed over whether its permanent home would be Saybrook, Wethersfield, or New Haven. In 1716 the college was finally located in New Haven by a decree of the General Assembly.

About that time a retired official of the East India Company made a donation to the college—"three trunks of textiles, muslins, calicoes, poplins, silk crepes and 'camletts'"—with the understanding that it would henceforth be named after him. So the name "Collegiate School" was changed to "Yale College," after Elihu Yale.

Throughout the eighteenth century Yale remained primarily a conservative school for the training of young men planning to enter the ministry, yet some of its graduates became the most influential men of their time and held positions of public responsibility and honor, not only in Connecticut but in many other colonies and even in England itself.

Farmers, Artisans, and Manufacturers

In the first decades of the early settlements the virgin soil was quite fertile because of the rich layer of old, decayed leaves and other particles from the thick forests that covered the land. Later the soil of Connecticut, outside the river valleys and the coastal areas, tended to become submarginal in quality. The land, especially in the eastern, northern, and western parts, was hilly, rugged, and generally unsuited for farming. Animals could be grazed on it, however, and the forest yielded wood and wood products.

Although the farm families were large, there never seemed to be enough hands for the work to be done. For major jobs such as house building or barn raising, neighbors helped each other.

Farming in colonial days was highly inefficient. The seed was poor, the tools primitive and clumsy. The chief grain crop was maize, or Indian corn. Wheat was introduced early in the eighteenth century, but it was subject to disease and blight and never became a popular crop. Connecticut farms also grew rye, oats, barley, flax, and hemp.

The chief vegetables were beans, peas, squash, turnips, and pumpkins. Wethersfield grew its famous onions for export, but other root crops were not generally used as food. Potatoes, for instance, were grown principally as cattle food. Fruit trees and berry bushes were plentiful, apples being a favorite because they could easily be turned into cider and applejack, or apple brandy.

In general, the farmers practiced extensive farming—that is, they applied small amounts of labor to large land areas and used little or no fertilizer.

Threshing grain on the barn floor with flails was practiced on farms in colonial Connecticut.

Animals were allowed to roam freely and range over the farmer's land in all kinds of weather, because it was believed that such treatment would build resistance to hardship. But farmers thereby lost the benefit of their dung. Oxen were used as the main sources of power for plowing and hauling, although toward the end of the seventeenth century more and more horses were being employed.

Men unable to make an adequate living on marginal farms began to put their other talents to work and became artisans. All the traditional crafts provided opportunities for a profitable sideline. Every town needed at least one weaver, carpenter, blacksmith, tanner, shoemaker, wheelright, and stonemason, and these craftsmen always needed helpers. Men without tools or skills sold their labor with little difficulty.

Every home had a spinning wheel, and every housewife knew how to spin, but not all had looms or knew how to weave. Every community needed at least one full-time weaver, to supply it with cloth of linen or wool. The housewives took the finished cloth and made it into clothes for their

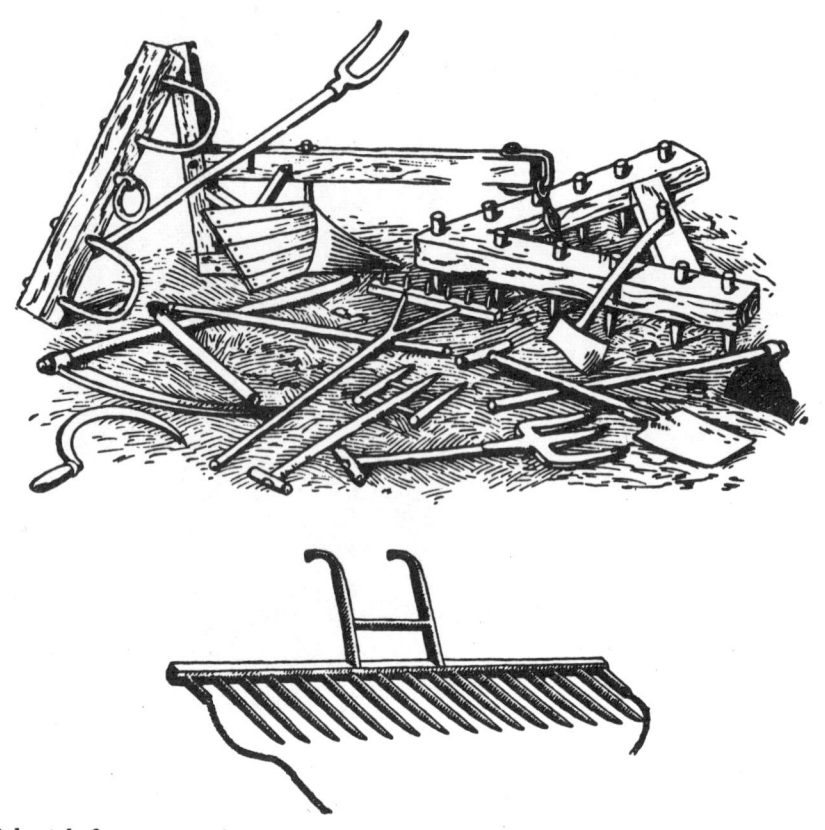

Colonial farming tools were primitive and inefficient. The New England farmer had to produce most of the items he needed himself.

families. When the richer members of a community began to seek better-fitting garments with more style and comfort, tailors joined the list of artisans. As early as 1697, a professional tailor was part of the community of Farmington.

The gristmill was usually the first manufacturing enterprise established in a town. A brook or stream would be dammed up to make a millpond, and then the mill would be erected beside it, the millwheel occupying the sluice, or exitway for the water. When the miller wished to grind grain, he opened the sluice gate. This released the water, and the water turned the wheel.

There were three kinds of millwheels. In early days men used an undershot wheel. Water simply flowed under this wheel and turned it clockwise by the force of its current. An improvement on the undershot wheel was the breast wheel. This wheel was so placed that the water flowed into it at midpoint, then down; the water still ran under the wheel and turned it clockwise, but the current's force was supplemented by the weight of gravity. The final development in millwheels was the overshot wheel. Water was conducted to this device by means of a millrace, or artificial channel, which carried it over the top of the wheel; it was turned counterclockwise and mainly by the force of gravity. In a dry season, when streams were down to a slow trickle, breast and undershot wheels could not be worked. But an overshot wheel took very little water to run and was an all-season device.

Inside the mill, a series of heavy wooden gears changed the millwheel's vertical revolutions into horizontal ones and operated the grinding stones. There were two of these, and they came in matched pairs—stones from two different sets did not grind well together. The lower stone, called the bedder, was fixed in place; the upper, called the runner, revolved. The threshed grain was poured into a large-mouthed hopper on top, from which it ran down into the stones. These were faced, or cut, in grooves, so that the ground flour was forced toward the outer rim, where it flowed out and was bagged. Legislation, passed in the 1660's, established the miller's fee as one twelfth of each bushel of corn he ground and one sixteenth of other grains.

After a gristmill, a sawmill was the most important factory to a colonial community. In a sawmill, the gears were so arranged that they operated a heavy frame, which moved up and down, something like the sash of a modern window. This frame contained a gang saw—that is, a series of saw blades set parallel to one another and as far apart as the desired thickness of the finished plank. An entire tree trunk could be fed into this device, drawn toward the saw blades by a ratchet, and emerge as a pile of planks. The machinery was not nearly so fast as modern power saws, of course—it was 1814 before even the first circular saw was invented —but it was a vast improvement over hand sawing.

Iron ore, discovered first in the New Haven and New London areas, enabled John Winthrop, Jr., to establish the first foundries. He and

Stephen Goodyear set up a forge and mill for rolling balls of iron near New Haven. These were in operation for a number of years. In 1728 Joseph Higley took out a patent on a process for making steel and was given a monopoly for ten years. Later good deposits of iron ore were located in the northwestern part of the colony, the most important mines being near Salisbury and Lime Rock. About 1748 a forge was erected at Lakeville, and in 1762 the first blast furnace was built. At the time of the Revolution the iron industry was well established, so that cannon and shot, gun barrels and chains were produced for use by the army and navy.

A rich vein of copper ore was found in Simsbury and Granby about 1705. Since the British government discouraged production of copper in the colonies, there were no native American specialists in smelting and refining ore. Undaunted, Connecticut mine owners hired German workmen and went into production in defiance of the British restrictions. Coins made from this ore in 1737 and 1739 circulated as legal tender for many years. Inscribed on some of the coins was the legend enclosed in two circles, "Value Me as you please" and on others, "I am good copper." Work at the Simsbury mines was carried on at intervals for more than seventy years, sometimes by free labor, sometimes by slave labor, and, after the establishment of Connecticut's Newgate Prison, by prison labor.

In the 1740's two Irishmen, Edward and William Pattison, skilled in the art of shaping tin into small ware, began a business in the town of Berlin, which became identified with the famous Yankee peddler. Their goods, eagerly bought as luxuries, replaced the crude wooden cups, bowls, and utensils that had been used previously.

Shipbuilding began early in Connecticut, for the first settlements were on rivers or on the shores of Long Island Sound, and there was plenty of lumber close by. Practically every port was a shipbuilding center, producing a great variety of vessels, some for coastal and river traffic and others for the profitable West Indies trade. Shipbuilding required a lot of hard work, for there were no appliances for bending timbers, and the planks, bolts, spikes, and nails all had to be made by hand. But Connecticut vessels were popular. Many shipping firms in England had their sloops and brigs built in New England.

Ship launchings were popular social events, with plenty of rum and perhaps a ball in the evening. When the vessels sailed, it was the custom to offer prayers for their safe return, and on their return, to offer thanks for their safety, because shipwrecks were frequent and the loss of lives and cargoes costly.

Most Connecticut farmers tried to be self-sufficient. The surplus products the farmer could spare for the market depended upon the location of his land and his ability and good luck at cultivating it. Although he and his family lived comfortably, they lived frugally. New Englanders held to a stern rule:

> Use it up, wear it out,
> Make it do, or do without.

The average farmer, however, had to purchase some things—those items he could not produce himself. Because of a serious shortage of coins, almost every purchaser bought on credit, but only someone well known to the merchant was trusted. The village or country storekeeper carried a wide variety of items, including spices, sugar, molasses, rum, many kinds of cloth and dress goods, crockery and glassware, powder, shot, and guns. The farmer in turn paid for these items with his surplus products: corn and other grains, cheeses, tallow, lard, hoops and staves, horses, cattle, vegetables, apples, and cider.

The local merchants sold the farm products to other merchants of the larger coastal or river towns. The town merchants in turn forwarded their surplus goods to the major ports of Boston, Providence, Newport, or New York, where they obtained their goods. In return they got supplies of European and West Indian goods to pass back up the line.

The town merchants profited from the country trade. The expanding markets matched Connecticut's population growth and in turn stimulated new commercial ventures.

The famed Yankee peddlers were often unpopular with the local merchants, who felt they sold inferior products at inflated prices. In 1765 the General Assembly raised the peddlers' license fee from £5 to £20 and provided a penalty for selling without a license.

Transportation improved with the greater flow of goods, and from 1700 to 1750 dozens of new roads linked the towns east of the Connecticut River to the markets in Providence, Boston, and Hartford. The coastal towns also enlarged their harbors, wharves, and warehouses. The opportunities for making wealth increased with the growth of trade, and many

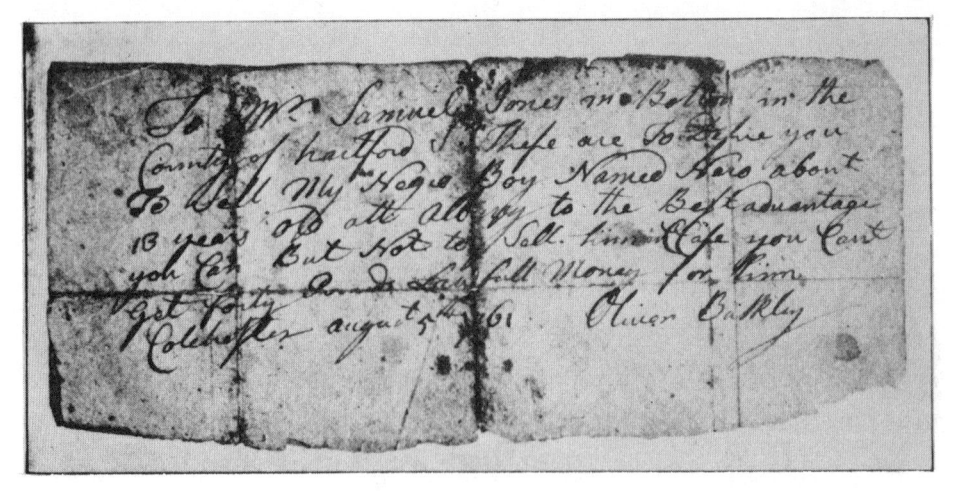

An original order for the sale of a Negro boy in New England in 1761. Slavery was still universal in the American colonies at this time.

a poor man was able to acquire a small fortune through shrewd trading and hard work.

Slavery

The Puritans accepted slavery as one of the facts of the age in which they lived. They found sufficient justification for slavery in the Bible, where it is also taken for granted. Slavery as it developed in Connecticut in the seventeenth and eighteenth centuries was a natural outcome of the heritage, customs, and religion of the people. The rightfulness of slavery was never seriously questioned.

Indian slavery had started after the Pequot War. The Code of 1650 sanctioned both Indian and Negro slavery. The Indians, however, did not make good slaves. They were not easily managed and tended to run away or cause problems or die. In early days the number of Negroes in Connecticut was very small, but after 1700 the black population gradually increased, as it did throughout the British colonies. The British government found that there were great profits to be made in the slave trade. Connecticut did not take part in the slave trade on a large scale, but some of the colony's sea captains did engage in it, and public auction sales were held there in which Negroes were bought and sold. The custom of holding men in bondage might have come to an end by the mid-eighteenth century had it not been for the importation of black Africans by Yankee ship owners.

The average slaveholder in Connecticut owned only one or two slaves. They were generally members of the household whom the master was required to care for and protect. Slaves performed household tasks or worked in the fields side by side with their masters. The slaves were servants for life, of course, but the law protected their rights to life and property, and, like the indentured servant, they had the privilege of suing masters for unjust treatment. The responsibility of their Christian upbringing was a serious matter, and many of the clergy owned one or two slaves as house servants.

The Great Awakening

The growth of religious indifference spread throughout New England until December 1734, when the Reverend Jonathan Edwards began a religious revival directed against the prevailing mood. His crusade won many converts and set the stage in Connecticut for the dynamic evangelism of George Whitefield and James Davenport.

Whitefield, a young English preacher, came to Connecticut in October 1740 and delivered sermons throughout the colony. Thousands heard him preach. His dramatic religious eloquence and his booming voice swept his listeners off their feet. Many ministers felt hostile toward him, whereas others were aroused to enthusiasm and cooperated eagerly in promoting the revival. The clerical leaders of the Great Awakening in Connecticut were a close-knit group, some related by blood or marriage, others by friendship, and this broad acquaintanceship was useful to the great preacher.

The most extravagant and influential of the followers of Whitefield was James Davenport, the great-grandson of the founder of New Haven. He was wildly eccentric in his preaching, and although he succeeded in converting many, his behavior finally led to his arrest as a vagrant and his return to his parish on Long Island.

The revival spread like wildfire in the years 1740, 1741, and 1742. Most places in the colony rejoiced in the large additions to their church membership. During some of the revival sermons, hysterical actions of all kinds occurred: "screachings, crying out," bodily contortions, jumping, dancing, visions, trances, and faintings. To some these were surely the work of divine favor, but to the staid older Puritans they were "the work of Satan," for the revivals embarrassed the regular conservative clergy by their unorthodox and violent appeals to emotion.

The main result of the Great Awakening was the formation of two "warring" factions, the Old Lights and the New Lights. The Old Lights opposed the movement, and the New Lights favored it. Representatives of each group were found everywhere, and the ministers were about equally divided. Although the leading citizens tended to be Old Lights, the rank and file of the New Lights were "chiefly of the lower and Younger Sort." The differences that separated the Old Lights and the New Lights were similar to the differences that separated the Church of England and the Puritans more than a hundred years before. To the New Lights, their opponents were upholders of a cold, lifeless religion while the defenders of the old order felt that the preachers of the Awakening were unreasoning fanatics, who were a menace to the social and moral order.

The Reverend George Whitefield was a preacher of the evangelical revival in both Great Britain and America. His influence on religious life was enormous and his work underlaid the foundation of as many as fifty colleges and universities in the United States.

In 1742 "an Act for regulating Abuses" was passed by the General Assembly to suppress the supposed excesses of the Awakening. This, however, served only to heap fuel on the fire of enthusiasm of the New Light ministers, who, when shut out of their meetinghouses, preached in private homes and out-of-doors. In time even some of the Old Lights felt the authorities went too far in repressing the activities of the New Lights.

The Great Awakening stirred the religious life of the colony to its depths. From the ferment came a new social and moral revolution that encouraged religious liberty and equality. This movement was further advanced by the events of the Revolutionary War and led finally in 1818 to the disestablishment of the Congregational Church.

The Susquehannah Company

Between 1730 and 1750 more than three thousand acres of land in western Connecticut opened for settlement, and by 1750 the last of these public lands was settled. Much of the farm land in the eastern part of the colony had declined in productivity while the population was steadily increasing. Many of the younger sons of the eastern farmers began to look outside the boundaries of Connecticut for new lands to settle on. By 1756 census figures revealed the population of Connecticut to be 126,975 whites, 3,019 Negroes, and 617 Indians. However, New London County was the only one of the six counties to count the Indians, so this figure is hardly an accurate census of the colony's Indian population. The increase in population in the years prior to 1756 was attributed to "industrious, temperate life and early marriages."

The Charter of 1662 gave Connecticut a claim to lands to the west all the way to the South Sea, and so, in the interest of developing new lands to the west, the Susquehannah Company was formed in 1753. The following year the agents of this company signed a treaty with certain Indian chiefs in western Pennsylvania, which gave them title to land along the Susquehanna River. If this title had been approved by the British government, the entire northern third of the colony of Pennsylvania would have come under the control of Connecticut.

The proprietors of Pennsylvania were opposed to the Susquehannah claim, naturally, but so were the settlers in western Connecticut. These people felt little urgent need for new lands and were afraid that the aggressive activities of the Susquehannah Company might cause the royal government to revoke the colony's famous charter, which allowed Connecticut so much self-government.

In 1763 the British government specifically prohibited the Susquehannah Company from making any settlements in Pennsylvania in the immediate future, but the supporters of the company hoped that the government would eventually change its mind. The disagreements over the Susquehannah issue and the issue of expansion beyond the historical boundaries of the colony remained a source of controversy and bitterness in the political life of Connecticut for many years.

Because its original Puritan leaders believed in the rule by the "elect" —those "chosen" by God for special favor, namely, church members— colonial Connecticut operated more like a republic than a democracy. Religious and property qualifications determined who should and could vote and rule. An aristocracy of First Families developed, for it is estimated that in 1766 only one ninth of the adult white male population qualified for this right.

A small number of families, mostly from the older established towns, controlled the government of the colony, and because of this Connecticut enjoyed remarkable political stability for the century prior to the end of the French and Indian War. From 1659 to 1766 only nine governors served, as governors were reelected annually and usually served until their death. Secretaries and treasurers of the colony also served lengthy terms. Three generations of one family held the same post for a total of ninety-eight years. Hezekiah Wyllys served as secretary of the colony for twenty-three years; he was succeeded by his son George, who served sixty-one years; and he in turn was succeeded by his son Samuel, who served fourteen years.

The Great Awakening and the Susquehannah Company issue, however, brought this political unity to an end, and political divisions along religious, geographic, and economic lines developed in the years just prior to the Revolution.

CHAPTER SEVEN

Prelude to the Revolution

In 1689, the year after William and Mary took the English throne, a series of wars began between England and France. This struggle for the balance of power in Europe was to last until the downfall of Napoleon in 1815.

On the European continent, France, with her far larger population and her geographic position, had the edge. But overseas England's commercial interests and superior sea power gave her an advantage. The question, over which the two nations were at war, was whether England could hold her own in Europe while she developed her overseas colonies.

In the first of these clashes, King William's War, Connecticut participated along with Massachusetts and New York. Most of the fighting centered around Albany, New York, where a series of raids by the French and their Indian allies spread panic throughout the northern colonies. An attack on Canada was planned, under the leadership of Fitz-John Winthrop, the governor's son. But when his troops had marched as far north as Lake Champlain, they were halted by an outbreak of smallpox and a lack of supplies, and had to turn back. The treaty of peace signed in 1697 merely provided that England and France would hold the same territory they had at the beginning of the war.

Five years later war again broke out. Anne was queen of England by then, so the war was called Queen Anne's War, and Spain joined France against England. In this conflict Connecticut's main concern was an invasion from the north by the French and their Indian allies. In the early morning of February 29, 1704, they attacked the village of Deerfield, Massachusetts, on the upper reaches of the Connecticut River, killed forty men, women, and children, and marched the 111 survivors to Canada through the deep winter snows. Four years later, Haverhill, Massachusetts, only thirty miles from Boston, suffered the same fate. Connecticut could hardly expect to escape forever.

In 1709, a major expedition was planned against Canada, supported by some regular troops plus levies from Massachusetts, New York, New Jersey, Pennsylvania, and Connecticut. The colonial troops were to assemble in Albany, then push on north to Champlain and down the lake toward Montreal. Meanwhile, a cooperating squadron of Royal Navy vessels would pick up another colonial army at Boston and proceed to Quebec by way of the St. Lawrence River, and the two forces would meet and conquer the French.

That was the plan. The colonies involved duly raised their troops, supplied them, armed them, sent them to the rendezvous, and there they waited. And waited and waited and waited, coming down with diseases and using up the precious supplies. The promised fleet did not appear, and it was October before the colonists were informed that the government in London had changed its mind. In disgust, the colonial troops disbanded and went home.

The following year, however, a promised fleet did appear, took aboard a New England force of 3,500 men and headed for Port Royal in French Acadia (modern Nova Scotia). This port, which had provided shelter for privateers who preyed on Yankee ships, had been a thorn in New England's side for generations, so Connecticut men were glad to assist in seizing it and the area around it. Renamed Annapolis Royal, it became an important base for the Royal Navy. Acadia in time would provide a foothold for ultimate British victory over French Canada.

All in all, Connecticut furnished over seven hundred men to serve in this war. The expense of supporting them was so great that it became necessary, for the first time, to issue paper money.

The third colonial conflict, King George's War, started out as a war with Spain, and several joint military-naval expeditions were launched against Spanish possessions in Florida and Central America. Mostly they were disastrously unsuccessful, plagued with tropical disease and the ineptitude of their leaders. Connecticut again raised its share of the one thousand New Englanders who were sent out to attack these strongholds. Fewer than a hundred of them returned.

Then in May 1744, word came that France had joined the war on Spain's side. That was the worst possible news for New England. The backcountry could expect raids from French-led Indians, the seacoast could expect privateering assaults on every Yankee vessel that stuck its bowsprit out of port. But it also offered an opportunity to get rid of another French thorn-in-the-side: the fortress of Louisbourg on Cape Breton Island.

Under the enterprising leadership of Massachusetts Governor William Shirley, the enterprise took shape. Three thousand New England troops, supported by a squadron of the Royal Navy, were to land at Canso (an island off the most easterly point of the Nova Scotian mainland), and from there launch a joint attack on the fortress. The field command was given to a merchant of Kittery, Massachusetts (now Maine), named William Pepperrell. Appointed second in command of the expedition was Connecticut's deputy governor, Roger Wolcott.

For once everything went as planned. On March 24, 1745, the first contingent set off from Boston for Nova Scotia and reached Canso on April 4. Two weeks later the naval squadron arrived and proceeded on to Louisbourg, to clamp a blockade around the fortress. In April the Connecticut contingent set off for Canso in a convoy of seven transports guarded by the Rhode Island sloop *Tartar*.

En route they were spotted by the French frigate *Renommée*. Skillfully the Rhode Islander lured the Frenchman away from the convoy, and the Connecticut troops escaped. Then after dark, eluding the *Renommée*, the *Tartar* rejoined her charges, and they proceeded on to Canso.

With Wolcott's contingent added to his own, Pepperrell ordered the expedition on to Louisbourg. By May 1 they had all landed within two miles of the fortress. Almost immediately they captured a large outwork, filled with huge siege guns, which the French had abandoned. With Yankee ingenuity they had these in working order within three days and turned them on their former owners. Soon the bombardment began in earnest. Pepperrell later reported, "We gave them about nine thousand cannon balls and six hundred bombs." On June 17, Louisbourg surrendered.

It was a great day for all New Englanders. They had defeated their

The *Connecticut Courant,* founded in 1764, is still in publication today as the *Hartford Courant.* The *Courant* became a leading patriotic newspaper after 1770, and often carried political propaganda and satire.

old enemy without the help of a single redcoat. But three years later, their joy was turned to anger and chagrin when word came that the Treaty of Aix-la-Chapelle, ending the war, had returned Louisbourg to the French in exchange for Madras, India.

The people of Connecticut, seeing that nothing had been gained by the heavy losses of men and the increase in their public debt, began to feel that the affairs of the colonies should be managed in America rather than by Parliament.

Colonial Newspapers

Just as the printing press played an important role in the Reformation in Europe, the establishment of colonial newspapers in Connecticut helped to influence events of the Revolutionary period.

The first newspaper was the *Connecticut Gazette,* founded in New Haven in 1755 by James Parker. New Haven at that time had a population of about five thousand inhabitants. The first issue was modest, only four pages, each six by ten inches—as wide as this page and slightly longer. There was very little news in that first issue, but the subscribers were promised they would receive weekly the latest news, articles of an educational value, and advertising service at reasonable rates.

Since the *Gazette* started publishing during the French and Indian War, it carried the latest news of the military campaigns. When the war ended, its public support declined, and it ceased publication in April 1764. A year later Benjamin Mecom, a nephew of Benjamin Franklin, brought the paper back to life as an outspoken champion of colonial rights. He was not as successful as his uncle, however, and the paper was again discontinued in February 1768.

In 1758 Timothy Green started the second newspaper in order of founding, the *New-London Summary, or the Weekly Advertiser*. This newspaper, the first of many to be printed by the Green family, relied heavily on war news and was similar in makeup to the New Haven *Gazette*. Although the *Summary* was also discontinued at the end of the French and Indian War, another Timothy Green, a nephew, began the *New London Gazette*, one of the few early papers to outlive the eighteenth century. Other newspapers were started in Hartford, Norwich, Middletown, and Litchfield, but except for the Hartford paper their life-spans were relatively short.

The oldest paper in continuous operation, the *Connecticut Courant* (still published today as the *Hartford Courant*), was founded in October 1764 by another member of the Green family, Thomas Green. Thomas had worked in his grandfather's printshop in New London and had been in charge of Parker's press in New Haven for several years until the *Gazette* was sold to Mecom.

Green then moved to Hartford so he could set up his own business. He installed his press on the second floor over a barbershop across the street from the State House and near Flagg's and Bull's taverns, favorite places for the politicians during the sessions of the General Assembly. Green's shop provided a wide variety of goods and services. Besides printing and the newspaper, "his shop served as a bookstore and stationer's, where Hartford people could buy primers, spelling books, bibles, copies of Watt's psalms, catechisms, quill pens, inkstands and so on." He also offered some household wares.

The early newspapers rarely contained editorials like those in modern newspapers, but the publisher was able to mold public opinion by his selection of materials. The *Connecticut Gazette* gave prominence to the relations between the colonies and Great Britain. It insisted that American problems be dealt with by Americans rather than by Englishmen three thousand miles away. This became a major theme of the newspapers throughout the Revolutionary period, as they aired the grievances, imagined or real, of the colonists. Though the actual number of subscribers to any one newspaper was small, its readership was much larger.

The *Courant* began with a cautious editorial policy under Green, but when his successor, Ebenezer Watson, took over in 1770, the paper became more outspoken on the points at issue between America and Great Britain. In fact, the paper became "recklessly critical of the English government."

The paper carried relatively little local news because everyone in town knew what had happened to his neighbors. The news from London appeared about two months after the events, Philadelphia items were two weeks late, and those from Boston and New York four or five days late. Since there was no system for news collection—no reporters, no legmen, no foreign correspondents—the editor had to rely on whatever news reached him accidentally through letters sent by friends and articles he could clip from other newspapers. Political propaganda and satire sometimes made up for a shortage of news. The paper also carried two or three columns of advertising each week. Humorous pieces appeared, and much space was devoted to scientific topics, particularly agriculture, mathematics, and astronomy. The paper represented the interests of its readers.

When Watson died in September 1777, his widow became probably the first woman editor in the country. Hannah Watson took as a partner George Goodwin, who had been associated with the *Courant* since he was a nine-year-old printer's devil, and in 1779 she married Barzillai Hudson. The partnership of Hudson and Goodwin became highly successful, and the *Courant,* under its woman editor, not only "supported the Revolution but advocated all sorts of moral and religious movements . . . with articles on temperance, cleanliness, and the happy effects of feminine society on men."

The *Courant* probably had about five hundred weekly subscribers in its early years, six hundred during the Revolution, and two thousand or more by the end of the century. During the Revolution there was some regular reporting, and during the Constitutional Convention, two of Connecticut's delegates, Roger Sherman and Oliver Ellsworth, wrote at length on the Federal Constitution. Whereas the *Courant* began its career as a radical newspaper, after the Revolution it tended to become more noticeably conservative.

Colonial printshops did much more than just print newspapers. Many published books as well. Occasionally a printer might contract to run off a colony's issue of paper money. At the very least, a thriving shop would print advertising broadsides, public notices and proclamations, lottery tickets—lotteries were a popular way to finance churches, schools, and public works—and especially an almanac. A useful guide to seamen and farmers and others who needed information about the weather, tides, stars, sun and moon, and so on, an almanac also served as a kind of magazine, containing witty sayings, sage advice, verse, and almost anything else the printer could think of. A successful almanac could make a printer wealthy, as *Poor Richard's* did Benjamin Franklin.

Most printing equipment came from England—the press, the type, the best paper. Only ink was easily made in the colonies, from lamp black and linseed oil. Until 1769 the complicated mechanism called a printing press was beyond the scope of American mechanics to produce. But in that

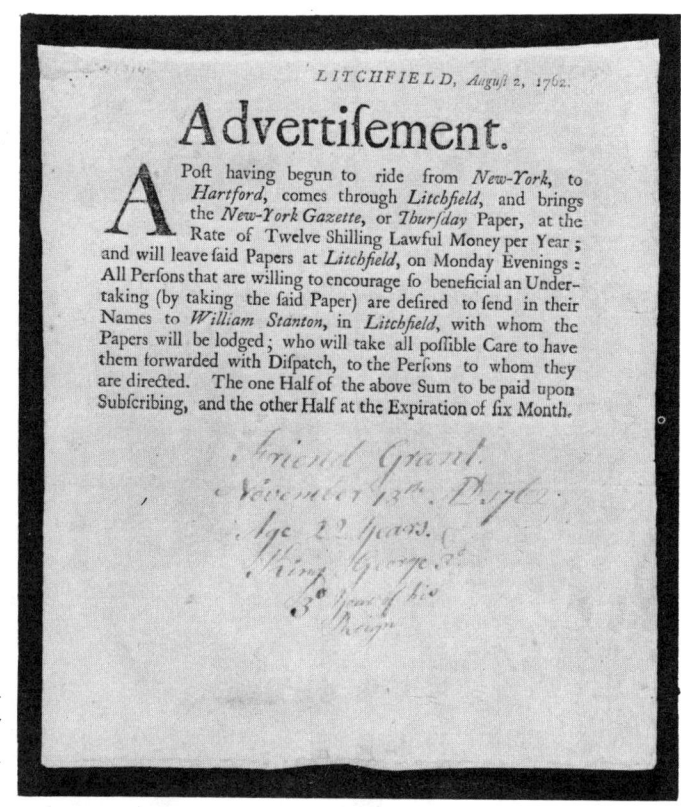

Getting subscribers was a problem even for the early newspapers. This is a 1762 ad for the *New-York Gazette*.

year, Isaac Doolittle of New Haven, Connecticut, sold the first American-made press to a Philadelphia printer—just in time for independence.

In that same year, also in Connecticut, a silversmith in Killingworth named Abel Buell was granted £100 to continue his experiments in type founding. Type was in great demand among colonial printers. In those days a font of type (all the necessary letters and punctuation for a particular style of type face in a particular size) was very small, with only limited numbers of *l*'s and *m*'s and so on. The type for a page had to be broken up as soon as the requisite number of copies had been run off, for it would be needed for setting the next page. Buell's early attempts were crude and failed, but by 1781 he was producing acceptable type for the Green family of printers.

Paper was somewhat more readily available in the colonies than type. By the time of the Revolution, there were paper mills in Connecticut, Massachusetts, Rhode Island, New York, Virginia, and North Carolina. The quality was low compared to fine European papers, however, and for elegant printing men preferred to import their paper.

A master printer usually employed several assistants—one or two journeymen plus a printer's devil, or apprentice. There was a lot to be done. Type was set by hand in a little wooden holder called a compositor's stick, and the setter had to be able to read upside down and backward, in order to set the material correctly.

When enough type had been assembled for a page, it was inked with a round, leather-covered, cushionlike device called an ink ball, and a "proof," or sample, was run off. The printer then read it carefully for errors, corrected them, and "locked up" the completed page in an iron frame by wedging it firmly into position with blocks of wood. Then with two men working together, the page was put into the press and inked, and the handle of the device was pulled with all a man's strength, to make a strong impression, and then released. The page was removed, another sheet of paper placed in the press, and the process resumed until the run was finished. Then the next page would be set, and so on.

The Last Colonial War

The French and Indian War broke out in 1754, when the French attempted to establish control of the Ohio Valley and Virginia attempted to stop them. Two regiments of regulars under Major General Edward Braddock were sent out from Britain the following year to drive the French from the Forks of the Ohio (modern Pittsburgh). Instead, they were ambushed and disastrously defeated.

Stout old William Shirley, still governor of Massachusetts, had been appointed Braddock's successor. He decided to retaliate with counterstrokes against two French forts: Fort St. Frédéric at Crown Point on Lake Champlain and Fort Niagara on Lake Ontario. He himself was to lead the advance toward Niagara, and the Crown Point expedition was put under the command of Indian superintendent William Johnson. Johnson's second in command was Phineas Lyman, a Connecticut lawyer. Not one of the three had any military experience at all.

Shirley got bogged down almost immediately without even reaching Niagara and was eventually relieved of his command. But Johnson and Lyman fared better. With about 3,500 troops, mostly from New York and New England, and four hundred Iroquois, they headed up the Hudson River, built a supply depot at Fort Edward (where the carrying place between the river and Lake George began), and then headed north for Lake George. The plan was to build another fort at the head of the lake, then descend to Lake Champlain and their principal objective, Fort St. Frédéric.

But they were still engaged in building the fort when word came that a French force under Baron Ludwig August Dieskau was on the way to assault them. It was September 8, 1755. Johnson ordered out an advance unit of about a thousand men to stop the French, but Dieskau managed to ambush them and drive them back into camp. When he advanced to attack the camp itself, however, he found himself facing a bristling barricade of felled trees—branches toward him, forming the eighteenth-century equivalent of barbed wire—and cannon, great 18- and 32-pounders loaded with grape.

Johnson was down to a mere 1,700 men by then, but Dieskau had fewer than 1,500. Nevertheless, the French commander recklessly attacked his entrenched enemy, and soon the forest was resounding with a furious exchange, cannonfire for musketry. One of the first victims of the colonials' grapeshot was Dieskau himself, who toppled over with two wounds. One of the first victims of French bullets was Johnson, who took a ball in the thigh and immediately retired to his tent, leaving General Lyman to conduct the rest of the Battle of Lake George.

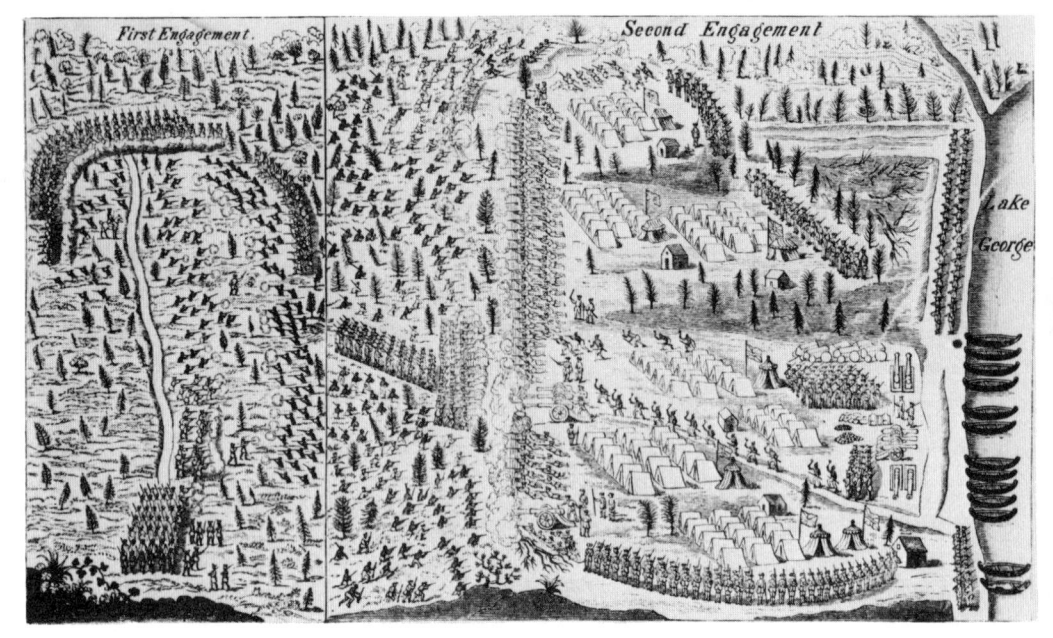

This old print shows the battles of Lake George. The site of several engagements during the French and Indian War, Lake George was originally called Lac St.-Sacrement by the French. William Johnson gave it its present name, in honor of the king, after defeating Baron Dieskau. That battle is represented as the first engagement. The second engagement refers to the routing of General Abercrombie by the Marquis de Montcalm in 1758.

It went on for hours. But eventually the Indians and Canadians among the French troops had had enough, and they began to desert. When he saw this, Lyman ordered a sortie. The soldiers left their entrenchments and, charging with hatchets, fell on the wavering French, who began to retreat. The colonials chased and harassed the enemy for four miles before giving up and returning to camp with their prisoners. Among the latter was Baron Dieskau himself, whom the Americans had found sitting groggily on a stump.

The retreating French force was subsequently caught by another American unit, moving up from Fort Edward to Lake George, and badly mauled. But no pursuit was ordered, and the enemy was permitted to retire safely to Crown Point. Too exhausted to complete their mission so late in the year, the colonials abandoned the advance toward the French fort and finished constructing their own, which they named Fort William Henry.

This map shows the region where the major battles occurred in the French and Indian War. In 1760 the war had ended in the American colonies, but fighting continued in Europe until the Treaty of Paris was signed in 1763.

Emboldened, the French moved farther south to erect a new fort at a place the Indians called Ticonderoga.

Nevertheless, the Battle of Crown Point was decisive. Along with Braddock's defeat at the Monongahela, it prodded Great Britain into launching a full-scale war against the French. (In its European and Far Eastern aspects, it was called the Seven Year's War.) Command of the fighting in America was taken from colonial officers and put in the hands of British professionals. And for his victory in this battle—he gave General Lyman no credit for his share it it—William Johnson was created a baronet and awarded £5,000.

For two years, Americans suffered from increasingly bold Indian raids, many following the familiar highway of the Connecticut River. A band of rangers, recruited largely from New Englanders, was formed under the leadership of New Hampshireman Robert Rogers. From his outpost on the upper river, Rogers scouted for the army and counterattacked against raiding Canadian Indians, and for many months his little group was the only effective protection the Valley people had. A succession of British commanders sent out from England did little to forward the war.

Meanwhile, the French were having brilliant success under Baron Dieskau's successor, a commander named Louis Joseph Marquis de Montcalm. Montcalm took Forts Oswego and William Henry—both surrenders followed by Indian massacres of unarmed prisoners—and then prepared to defend Canada itself against the attack that was coming.

For by 1758 the tide had begun to turn. For once the British government had not shirked its share and had shipped many regiments of regulars to the colonies to bear the brunt of the war. With their help, Fort Duquesne at the Forks of the Ohio was taken, as was the fortress at Louisbourg that the government had carelessly restored to French control ten years earlier. Shortly Forts Carillon (Ticonderoga) and Frédéric (Crown Point) were abandoned, and Wolfe was at the gates of Quebec. By 1760, when Montreal fell, it was all over.

It took three years more of fighting on the Continent and in India before Britain, France, and their allies signed the Treaty of Paris, ending the war. By its terms French Canada passed into English control, and New Englanders could expect a future free of Indian raids.

CHAPTER EIGHT

The Colony Is Aroused

For Connecticut the French and Indian War had involved greater numbers of men, heavier losses of life, and larger expenditures than all the previous wars. Nevertheless, in spite of the fact that one fifth of the able-bodied men between the ages of sixteen and forty-five had been removed from productive labor, Connecticut's economy remained strong. The war years actually brought prosperity, as large amounts of beef, pork, flour, wheat, and other items were sold to the militia and the British troops. But the end of the war brought a severe depression.

England emerged from the French and Indian War as the supreme power in the world. She controlled the North American continent from the Atlantic to the Mississippi River and from Hudson's Bay in the North to Florida in the South. The Mediterranean and the Caribbean came largely under British control, as did French possessions in Africa and India. The empire on which "the sun never set" was taking shape.

England also emerged from the wars greatly in debt. Taxes for the British people had doubled, and if the government was to maintain forces in America to control its newly won territories, alternative forms of taxation had to be found. King George III and his ministers concluded that the expense of the American defense should be raised by America itself. This seemed logical to them, and so the Sugar Act of 1764, the Stamp Act of 1765, and the Townshend Duties of 1767 were passed by Parliament in order to raise the necessary funds. England assumed that the colonists, as loyal subjects of the mother country, would accept the government's decision. However, this was not to be so in Connecticut, which was conditioned by a century of self-government and economic independence.

Operating under the Charter of 1662, Connecticut enjoyed more self-government than any other colony in North America, with the exception of Rhode Island. The local towns conducted their affairs with a minimum of interference from the colonial government, and the colonial government had the same arrangement with the royal government. In fact, Connecticut had relatively little direct contact, either politically or economically, with England during most of its first hundred years.

The colony protested the Sugar Act because of the effect it would have on the limited trade Connecticut had with the West Indies. The *Courant* in Hartford lamented that "our trade to the French and Spanish islands is stopped. . . . Merchants and farmers are breaking; and all things going into confusion." In spite of this lament, Connecticut was not as badly affected as were many of the other colonies; its ports were important mostly in the local coastal trade. Nevertheless, Governor Thomas Fitch prepared a reasoned protest and sent it off to London.

Jared Ingersoll

The outcry over the Sugar Act, which affected only a special portion of the population, was nothing compared to the protest aroused by the Stamp Act. The Stamp Act was felt by everyone. A direct tax, it required a special government stamp on all business papers, licenses, newspapers, college diplomas, marriage licenses, and other legal documents. It was a tax that struck hardest at the most vocal and most politically minded individuals in the colonies.

Jared Ingersoll, one of the most highly respected persons in Connecticut, found himself in 1765 in the middle of the controversy as the royal collector of the stamp tax. He had been born in Milford in 1722 and was graduated from Yale in 1742 as the winner of the Berkeley scholarship, which entitled him to an extra year of study. While at Yale he refused to become involved in the religious revivalism of the Great Awakening, and as a result he made many enemies as well as friends who were to influence his life in later years.

He began his political career in 1751 with an appointment as king's attorney for New Haven county. Because of his commitment to the established religious and social order, he was chosen in 1758 as the official agent for Connecticut in London. His association and friendship with many of the leaders in the British government helped to explain his sympathy for England's colonial policy. Furthermore, he was in London during the first year of George III's reign, when England was entering upon a new phase of its colonial policy, and he played a minor role in shaping that policy.

When Ingersoll returned to New Haven in the fall of 1761, he found that the religious differences of the Great Awakening had become part of the established political scene. Moreover, there was a growing division between the political and economic interests of the eastern and western parts of the colony.

Ingersoll's second tour of duty in England coincided with the passage of the Stamp Act in 1765. He and Benjamin Franklin, Pennsylvania's agent, presented the colonial objections to the tax and did all they could to remove the most objectionable aspects. In discussions with Parliament's leaders Ingersoll became convinced "that the stamp tax was both necessary and just." On the advice of Franklin he decided that he could best help Connecticut if he accepted the appointment as collector of the stamp tax,

The Stamp Act required that this stamp be used on all publications and legal documents. Opposition to the hated act took the form of newspaper editorials, organization of the Sons of Liberty, boycott of English goods, and the Stamp Act Congress. Parliament, fearing a loss in trade, repealed the Stamp Act in 1766.

and so Ingersoll became the "Stamp Master General for New England Colonies."

Opposition to the Stamp Act developed slowly but steadily in Connecticut under the leadership of the Sons of Liberty. This loose organization of workingmen, who had formed up in nearly every one of the thirteen colonies, took their name from a term used by Colonel Isaac Barré in a speech against the Stamp Act in Parliament. They were anti–Stamp Act and prone to violence. Ingersoll found, upon his return to New Haven, considerable opposition to the new tax. Although he attempted to persuade his fellow townsmen of the need for the tax, a town meeting in September called for his resignation as official stamp master.

In other parts of the colony, Ingersoll was being hanged in effigy. In Lebanon his effigy was tried and convicted by a jury, dragged through the village, and finally burned before a cheering throng. In Windham and Norwich, the Sons of Liberty held protest meetings, for they were most active in stirring up opposition to the Stamp Act in eastern Connecticut.

Ingersoll hoped that Governor Fitch, whose conservative views were similar to his own, would be able to persuade the General Assembly of the reasonableness of the tax and the need to avoid direct conflict with British authority and power. Therefore, shortly after the New Haven meeting Ingersoll set off for Hartford on horseback. For most of the miles after he left New Haven, he rode alone and unmolested, but by the time he reached Wethersfield, he had acquired an escort of several hundred horsemen armed with clubs and staves. The horsemen were Sons of Liberty, hastily organized to bring pressure upon Ingersoll and the General Assembly. They demanded that he resign his post as stamp collector immediately, but Ingersoll would not make that decision without consulting with the governor and the General Assembly.

The mood of the crowd, however, was such that they were unwilling to listen to reason. Tired from his ride, the middle-aged Ingersoll managed to shut himself up in a private home for more than three hours, but then, giving up hope of rescue or support, he signed an official statement of resignation that the Sons of Liberty had prepared. They forced him to read the statement to the crowd and to join in shouting their slogan, "Liberty and Property." Although Ingersoll did not lack personal courage, he saved himself personal abuse by giving in to popular pressures for his resignation.

The crowd, now having grown close to a thousand, then escorted Ingersoll to Hartford, where he was forced to repeat his declaration of resignation before the General Assembly and to reaffirm his commitment to "Liberty and Property."

The Easterners and the Westerners

The experience of Jared Ingersoll showed the extent to which the colony was divided in these troubled years. The general unhappiness with the new policies of the British government widened the division between the peoples of eastern Connecticut and those of the western portion.

During the summer of 1765 the leaders in eastern Connecticut had organized the Sons of Liberty with two objectives in mind. The first was to convince the freemen of Connecticut that their liberties could be secure only if the "Tories" of western Connecticut were removed from control of the colonial government. The term "Tory" was used to describe anyone sympathetic to Parliament and its policies or to the Church of England. The second objective was to organize the colony so as to elect Patriot leaders who would favor the eastern part of the colony. Their plan, when it was put into operation, proved more successful than even they expected.

That the two sections of the colony would react so differently to the colonial policies of the mother country was a reflection of their historical relationship with England. Eastern Connecticut, predominently rural and economically underdeveloped, expressed the traditional hostility of the Puritan founders toward Anglican England. They had little contact with London except by way of Providence, Newport, or Boston. So it is not surprising that the Connecticut Sons of Liberty were organized and most active in eastern Connecticut.

Western Connecticut, on the other hand, had a great deal of business contact with the royal colony of New York. It had been settled by many wealthier and more aristocratic elements and in recent years had controlled the government in Hartford. The Great Awakening drove many western residents into the security of the Church of England, which had a surprising growth of membership between 1740 and 1760. Though western Connecticut did not like the idea of paying any more taxes, they felt that Parliament was supreme and that Connecticut must obey the laws of the realm.

Another issue that divided the eastern and the western parts of the colony was that of paper money. The merchants of eastern Connecticut, hampered by a shortage of money, proposed to the General Assembly as early as 1730 the issuance of currency based on mortgages to be deposited with the "New London Society for Trade and Commerce." The General Assembly, controlled by the more populated western towns, did not respond favorably to the idea. The western merchants in reality feared the possible growth of competition from the eastern merchants, and so succeeded in destroying the New London Society, on the grounds that Parliament wanted to keep paper money out of circulation because it was so rarely backed by hard currency.

Thomas Fitch

The humiliation of Ingersoll was the Sons of Liberty's first political success. Their next victim was Governor Thomas Fitch, governor during the trying years of the French and Indian War.

Fitch, born in 1700 in Norwalk to one of the wealthiest families in western Connecticut, showed during his years at Yale "a fondness for . . . some of the doctrines" of the Church of England, even though he remained a Congregationalist. In fact, he preached in the Norwalk church when the church was without a regular minister.

After beginning his law career in Norwalk, he was elected to represent his home town in the General Assembly. In 1742 the General Assembly appointed him, along with Lieutenant Governor Roger Wolcott, Jonathan Trumbull, and John Bulkeley, to revise the laws of the colony. The others, for unknown reasons, contributed very little to the completed revision, which was regarded by English jurists as "the finest colonial code ever published." Fitch was also highly esteemed by his colleagues as "probably the most learned lawyer who had ever been an inhabitant of the colony."

In 1750 Fitch was chosen lieutenant governor and four years later had the distinction of being the first person in Connecticut to defeat an incumbent governor for that office. His popularity and influence became widespread during the French and Indian War.

The growing popularity of the Sons of Liberty, both throughout the colony and in the General Assembly, and their repeated demands for the

The Sons of Liberty brought about the downfall of Governor Thomas Fitch. He lost his reelection bid to William Pitkin.

repeal of the Stamp Act proved to be Fitch's political downfall. Having taken an oath to uphold the law, Fitch felt compelled to support the Stamp Act. The power of the Sons of Liberty, however, increased to the point where they assumed much of the authority regularly exercised by the government.

When Fitch came up for reelection in the spring of 1766, the Sons of Liberty campaigned against him by playing up the hard times Connecticut was then experiencing and the possible loss of its liberties because of the British taxation. Even though the Stamp Act was repealed in February 1766, the Sons of Liberty succeeded in getting their ticket of William Pitkin and Jonathan Trumbull elected by declaring that Connecticut needed leadership that would oppose any future British tyranny.

The Easterners Gain Control

Not only did the election bring the governorship and the upper house of the General Assembly under the control of the easterners, but they

This colonial cartoon depicts the burial of the Stamp Act in 1766.

maintained this control throughout the entire Revolutionary period. As a result Connecticut followed an unyielding Patriot line until the end of the Revolutionary War. Governor Pitkin served until his death in 1769, and then Trumbull served as governor until 1784.

With easterners in control in Hartford, the Susquehannah issue came to the forefront again. Governor Trumbull was openly in favor of the settlement of the cheap fertile lands of the Susquehannah claim by the land-starved eastern farmers. The General Assembly in January 1774 extended its authority over the Susquehannah claim in the Wyoming Valley of Pennsylvania, which was organized into the township of Westmoreland. Over two thousand settlers from Connecticut, with Governor Trumbull's blessing, migrated there. These actions brought strong objections from the conservative western opposition who feared that the charter would be endangered and so petitioned the General Assembly to revoke its Susquehannah decision. In the election of May 1774, however, the conservative element was soundly defeated and the expansionists scored a decisive victory.

When the Townshend Duties in 1767 imposed taxes on British imports, Connecticut's leadership, with the backing of the Sons of Liberty, wasted no time in objecting. Governor Pitkin filed a protest with London, stating that the new duties were a violation of Connecticut's charter-given privilege of being responsible for its own taxation. The Sons of Liberty, however, did not feel this was strong enough, and so they organized protest meetings in New London, Norwich, and Windham, in order to arouse public sentiment for the nonimportation and nonconsumption of British goods. The idea of nonimportation and nonconsumption, used also in other colonies, caused the British in 1770 to repeal all the Townshend duties except the tax on tea.

The news of the Boston Tea Party stirred Connecticut. The *Courant* carried the story in a single mocking sentence:

> We hear from Boston that last Thursday evening, between 300 and 400 Boxes of the celebrated East-India TEA, by some ACCIDENT! which happened in an attempt to get it on Shore, fell overboard— That the Boxes burst open and the Tea was swallowed up by the vast Abyss!

The conservative element was dismayed and greatly feared that Parliament would soon retaliate, but the Sons of Liberty showed their patriotism by burning some tea brought in by a peddler. When the Coercive Acts of 1774 closed the port of Boston until the tea dumped in the harbor was paid for, the General Assembly promised Boston aid "in its hour of trial." It accepted Virginia's invitation to set up a Committee of Correspondence to keep each of the colonies alert to patriotic activities and also named three active patriots, Roger Sherman of New Haven, Silas Deane of Wethersfield, and Eliphalet Dyer of Windham, to represent Connecticut in the First Continental Congress.

Among the thirteen colonies Connecticut ranked about in the middle in population with 7 to 8 percent of the total inhabitants. A census taken in 1774 showed 191,392 whites, 5,085 Negroes, and 1,363 Indians. The Indians were slowly dying out and for the most part lived peacefully on reservations, which the General Assembly had set up nearly a century before. The Negroes were mainly centered in the seaport towns along Long Island Sound. The rest of the inhabitants were almost entirely of English descent, although there was a scattering of Dutch, French Huguenots, and French Canadians. The most densely populated areas were along the coast of the Sound and in the river valleys; however, the Connecticut River Valley south of Middletown remained sparsely populated. Litchfield County, in the northwestern section, was Connecticut's last frontier.

As the momentum toward revolution increased, the patriots became more energetic in their activities. Many of the Tory sympathizers in western Connecticut were forced into silence or were hounded into New York, which was stronger in its allegiance to the Crown. Any opposition by the Tories received both popular and official denunciation. Governor Trumbull held that "a man's right to protection by the state was qualified by his political opinions." He believed it was not in his power to prevent people from doing what they considered to be their duty.

CHAPTER NINE

The Provision State

By late Saturday afternoon, April 22, 1775, the news of the battles of Lexington and Concord had spread throughout most of Connecticut. Like Paul Revere, who spread the alarm "through every Middlesex village and farm," a postrider, Israel Bissell of Watertown, Massachusetts, was ordered "to alarm the Country quite to Connecticut" and beyond. He rode so hard, in fact, that his horse fell dead in Worcester, but after some rest Bissell mounted a fresh horse and rode south into Connecticut. By Thursday evening he had spread the news to Norwich and New London and by riding all night he reached New Haven by Friday evening.

One of the Yale students, eighteen-year-old Ebenezer Fitch, recorded in his diary the reactions of the townspeople and the students:

> Friday, April 21. To-day tidings of the battle of Lexington, which is the first engagement with the British troops, arrived at New Haven. This filled the country with alarm, and rendered it impossible for us to pursue our studies to any profit.

Rumors of what happened at Lexington and Concord spread rapidly inland to Hartford. Five days after the battles the *Courant* printed a general account of the fighting based on "the latest accounts from Boston." Its readers learned:

> Last Tuesday night the Grenadiers and Light Companies . . . in Boston were ferried in long-boats from the bottom of the Common

over to Phip's farm in Cambridge, from whence they proceeded on their expedition to Concord. [The next morning at Lexington] they gave a specimen of their savage designs, by firing several times on a number of innocent men.

The *Courant* also reported that the Americans lost 32 or 33 men, whereas the British lost up to 200 Regulars.

The first eyewitness account of Lexington and Concord appeared in the May 8 edition of the *Courant* when the editor, Ebenezer Watson, printed Isaiah Thomas' famous account word for word. This account began with a patriotic exhortation and assumed that the readers knew something about the battle:

> WORCESTER, May 3. AMERICANS! forever bear in mind the BATTLE of LEXINGTON!—where British troops, unmolested and unprovoked, wantonly, and in a most inhuman manner fired upon and killed a number of our countrymen, then robbed them of their provisions, ransacked, plundered and burnt their houses! nor could the tears of defenseless women, some of whom were in the pains of childbirth, the cries of helpless babes, nor the prayers of old age, confined to beds of sickness, appease their thirst for blood!—or divert them from the DESIGN of MURDER and ROBBERY!

Within days after the battles, close to three thousand militiamen from all parts of Connecticut had organized and marched off to Boston. One of the first units to arrive was the Second Company of the Governor's Foot Guard under Captain Benedict Arnold.

Within a week the General Assembly met in special session, and Governor Trumbull urged upon the lawmakers, "Firmness, Steadiness, Deliberation & Unanimity in the most important Affair that ever came under Consideration within these Walls." The legislators directed the militia to organize and equip themselves for "the special defense and safety of this Colony" and placed restrictions on the export of provisions "except stores for vessels bound to sea." Military appointments were made; David Wooster was appointed a major general and Joseph Spenser and Israel Putnam were made brigadier generals of special troops.

In order to keep inflation under control, more than £50,000 in paper money was printed and a special sevenpence tax was passed. Because taxes were kept at a high level throughout the war, Connecticut was able to operate on a fairly efficient level of operation.

Israel Putnam

Israel Putnam, a colorful hero even before the Revolution began, had been a member of Roger's Rangers during the French and Indian War. In 1762 he commanded the contingent of 1,000 sent by Connecticut in the naval expedition against Havana. His vessel was wrecked off the Cuban coast, and he was one of the few survivors on board who escaped by rafts and took part in the successful attack on Havana. Active in the Sons of Liberty during the Stamp Act protest, he served several terms in the General Assembly and became chairman of the local Committee of Correspondence in the years prior to the break with England. When the port

Many popular legends grew up about the exploits of Israel Putnam, who was at various times a ranger, scout, and brigadier general, until a stroke in 1779 ended his military career. He died in 1790 in Pomfret, Connecticut.

of Boston was closed as a result of the Boston Tea Party, Putnam drove a flock of 125 sheep to Boston from his farm in Pomfret (now Brooklyn, Connecticut), in order to help in the food shortage. His tavern was a favorite meeting place for ex-soldiers. Putnam was a short man with broad shoulders and a large head covered by a shock of gray hair, and his frankness, courage, and geniality made him popular with the men who served

At the Battle of Bunker Hill he commanded a regiment made up largely of men from Windham and New London counties. He was all over the battlefield and is credited with two significant contributions: with moving his troops to Breed's Hill, where the Battle of Bunker Hill was actually fought, and with giving the order, "Don't fire until you see the whites of their eyes."

After Bunker Hill Connecticut soldiers continued to play a prominent part in the operations around Boston. The semitrained militiamen held their own against the best British troops, even though Connecticut's citizen-soldiers were unaccustomed to the needed discipline of military life and often acted irresponsibly.

When the Continental Army moved to New York, Washington put Putnam in command until his arrival. Washington liked Putnam, yet he was somewhat overwhelmed by Putnam's eagerness. Much of the blame for the American defeat in the Battle of Long Island, therefore, was placed upon Putnam, who was in charge of the important Jamaica Pass and failed to guard it properly.

After this defeat on Long Island in 1776, a serious morale problem developed, and the poorly disciplined American troops deserted in droves. Some 6,000 of Connecticut's militia of 8,000 deserted, and an observer commented:

> For as Well the Officers as the Men belonging to the Militia, behaved extreamly ill; and Officers of all Ranks & Privates kept deserting & running off, in a Most Shamefull Scandalous Manner, and some were taken sick and a great Many more pretended to be so.

The Summer Soldiers

One of General Washington's greatest problems throughout the war was the staying power of the troops. Desertion was rampant, and Connecticut's men were no different from the soldiers of other states in their desire to return home. Following the attack on Fort Ticonderoga by Ethan Allen and Benedict Arnold, Philip Schuyler wrote Governor Trumbull in October 1775 that the Connecticut troops "melted away," believing that their obligation had ended with the end of their enlistment period.

The General Assembly recognized that punishing these men would only hinder Connecticut in its task of filling its quota of troops. So in 1776 and 1777 it passed acts providing for pardons for those "summer soldiers" who resumed their military obligations. Throughout the war Governor Trumbull worked hard to raise troops for the American cause.

As long as they were engaged in the fighting, Connecticut's troops had admirable records. They took an active part in most of the significant engagements from the start of the northern campaign in 1775 around Boston until the final victory at Yorktown in 1781. With a population of about 200,000, Connecticut had almost 40,000 men in military service of some sort. Yet in 1777 Governor Trumbull wrote Washington that the job of recruiting men in Connecticut had become difficult because there was a "distrust for the service" as a result of the lack of food, clothing, shelter, and pay in the Continental Army.

Joseph Plumb Martin joined Captain Samuel Peck's Company in Milford in 1776, at the age of fifteen, as a private and served seven years with the Continental Army. Years later he described with lively humor the adventures, the miseries, and the sufferings of the day-to-day life of the common soldier who almost every night had to lie "on the cold and often wet ground without a blanket and with nothing but thin summer clothing. . . ." Martin would lie "on one side until the upper side smarted with the cold, then turn that side down to the place warmed by my body and let the other take its turn at smarting, while the one on the ground warmed." When the ground was covered with hoarfrost or when it rained all night, the soldiers would lie down and "take our musket in our arms and place the lock between our thighs and 'weather it out'."

Martin once encountered another Connecticut man in a lonely spot:

> Had I possessed the power of foreknowledge, I might . . . have put Arnold asleep without anyone knowing it and saved . . . my country much trouble and disgrace. . . . [It] was but three or four days before his desertion. I met him upon the road a little distance

from Dobbs Ferry; he was then taking his observations and examining the roads. I thought he was up to some deviltry. . . . He looked guilty, and well he might, for Satan was in as full possession of him at that instant as ever he was of Judas; it only wanted a musket ball to have driven him out. . . .

At the beginning of the war the General Assembly adopted a ration schedule for its troops that later served as a model for the Continental commissariat. The daily ration provided each soldier with three quarters of a pound of pork or one pound of beef, one pound of bread or flour, and three pints of beer. In addition, each man was supplied with "one jill [gill, half a cup] of rum to each man upon fatigue per day," along with milk, molasses, soap, candles, vinegar, coffee, chocolate, sugar, tobacco, onions, and vegetables. Each week's ration would also include a half pint of rice or a pint of cornmeal, six ounces of butter, and three pints of peas and beans.

Each town was allotted a fixed quota of supplies based on the town's assessed valuation. In general the record of the towns in supplying their allotments was excellent, and this was especially true during the terrible winter at Valley Forge in 1777–78. When more than two thirds of the troops were barefoot and thousands were without blankets, Washington wrote Governor Trumbull that

> among the troops unfit for duty and returned for want of clothing none of your State are included. The care of your legislature in providing clothing . . . for their men is highly laudable, and reflects the greatest honor upon their patriotism and humanity.

To the men in the field, however, the spector of hunger was always with them in spite of the best efforts of the people at home. Joseph Plumb Martin wrote that during the campaigns of 1780 "the monster Hunger, still attended us. He was not to be shaken off by any efforts we could use, for here was the old story of starving, as rife as ever." Martin and the other troops hoped that things would improve, and they did for a while as the soldiers were supplied with some "musty bread and a little beef, about every other day." However, the men had about reached the limits of their endurance and were ready to quit rather than starve to death.

It was a hard decision to make, for, as Martin pointed out, "they were truly patriotic, they loved their country, and they had already suffered everything short of death in its cause."

To most of the raw Connecticut recruits or even the battle-hardened veterans, the ideals of the American Revolution had little relevance. In most instances they had never been more than a few miles from home, very little actual fighting took place on Connecticut's soil, and, therefore, the concept of "the United States of America" as expressed in the Declaration of Independence had little meaning for them, or for many of the people at home.

The *Courant* carried the full text of the Declaration of Independence in its July 15 issue on page 2 in keeping with the custom of the time of printing the news in approximately the order in which it arrived at the printing office. The *Journal* of New Haven, which President Ezra Stiles of Yale complained was a Tory paper, "gave no prominence to the Declaration of Independence, but printed that famous statement . . . on the back page of [the] paper, surrounded by advertisements of West India rum, coffee, and pepper."

To encourage men to enlist for a full three-year period General Washington wanted a policy of bounties of both money and land. Two laws, passed by the General Assembly, aided the towns in filling their quota of enlistees as the war continued. One allowed any two men to hire another as their substitute for three years in the Continental Army, and the other allowed slave owners to emancipate their slaves so that they, along with free blacks and whites, could be hired as substitutes to fill part of a town's quota. As a result 289 black soldiers served in the war from Connecticut. Most of these received their freedom, although how many Connecticut slaves received their freedom for serving in the war is not known.

Nathan Hale

If the conduct of the deserters and the "summer soldiers" left much to be desired, then the example of men like Joseph Plumb Martin and Nathan Hale embodied all the noble sacrifices we associate with the American Revolution.

Nathan Hale, Connecticut's most famous and cherished Revolutionary hero, was born in Coventry in eastern Connecticut on June 6, 1755. He came from a large family, nine sons and three daughters, and his father, Deacon Richard Hale, was a successful farmer and zealous Patriot.

Hale entered Yale with his brother Enoch in 1769 at the age of fourteen. Excellent in his studies as well as successful in athletics, he soon adopted as his motto "Waste not a moment." Although his parents wanted him to become a minister, Hale preferred teaching school. After graduation he taught in East Haddam and New London. As a teacher he was exceedingly popular with his students. His athletic ability impressed the older boys, and his firm, decided manner gave him remarkable control with the other students.

When the war broke out, Hale secured a leave of absence from his teaching and joined the New London troops in Boston. Commissioned a first lieutenant, he gained the respect and love of the men under his command in the Seventh Connecticut Regiment. He participated in the siege of Boston during the fall and winter of 1775–76. By the time Washington moved his troops to Long Island, Hale had been promoted to captain in Knowlton's Rangers and had become a friend of General Washington.

Washington's troops, greatly outnumbered by the British and poorly equipped, were partially discouraged by their defeat in the Battle of Long Island. Washington, therefore, desperately needed information on the British plans. He called for a volunteer to go behind the British lines as a spy. Hale, eager for action and fully understanding the dangers involved in being caught as a spy by the British, volunteered for the mission.

Leaving the American camp at Harlem Heights, Hale and his close friend Stephen Hempstead of New London went to Norwalk, where they ferried across the Sound in the darkness to Huntington, Long Island. Dressed in his gray schoolmaster clothes and carrying his college diploma, Hale was determined to act the role of a teacher in search of a position.

What happened between the time he left Huntington and his capture is not documented. However, it is known that he mapped the British fortifications and wrote out in Latin full and accurate information about all he saw and heard. With these materials hidden in his shoes, he started on his way back to the American lines but was recognized by a Tory relative, who reported his presence.

He was apprehended by the British on September 21, 1776, and sent to the headquarters of General Howe in New York for questioning. There

Nathan Hale exemplifies the best traditions of the Revolutionary War heroes and is still revered as a martyr.

"he at once declared his name, his rank in the American Army, and his object in coming within the British lines." Although Howe admired the brave and courageous Hale, the rules of war showed no mercy for spies, and so he was ordered to be hanged at sunrise the next morning. Before he was hanged in the presence of several king's officers, Hale spoke the words for which he was to become famous: "I only regret that I have but one life to lose for my country."

Newgate

Connecticut has the dubious honor of having housed the Revolution's most noxious prison—the American counterpart of the infamous hulks, where the British imprisoned captured rebels in the fetid holds of ships. Newgate, as it was called after London's famed prison, was simply the Simsbury copper mines.

The copper mines, situated on the side of a hill in what is now East Granby, consisted of two vertical shafts, one seventy feet, the other thirty-five feet deep. From the bottoms of these diggings, horizontal tunnels had been excavated in several directions, as the ore was found. In 1773 the colony installed a grill over the mouth of the deeper tunnel, about six feet below the surface, and began to send convicted burglars and counterfeiters there, to serve their terms mining ore.

After the war broke out, the Patriot party started using Simsbury as a jail for Tories—men whose offense against the Revolution was as serious as treason. They were sent down the shaft into the bowels of the mine and ordered to dig ore. No food was supplied them—that had to be brought them by their friends. A blockhouse was raised over the mouth of the shaft, and a pair of sentries were left to guard it.

The mine had a fearsome reputation throughout the colonies and even abroad as an escape-proof and dreadful place to be incarcerated, and important or dangerous prisoners were often sent there from other colonies. But this name for maximum security was largely mythical, for the mine was plagued by fires—probably set by prisoners—and escapes. The wooden blockhouse was burned out repeatedly, and once a heavy wooden gate that closed off the exit of a water drain was lighted by some would-be escapees, only to come close to killing them with smoke in the narrow tunnel.

After one such fire, the mines were closed for three years while repairs were made and the blockhouse strengthened. But a few months after it was reopened, prisoners staged the biggest breakout of all.

At ten in the evening, May 18, 1781, the wife of a prisoner named Young appeared and asked to see him. There were only two guards on duty, and one of them had apparently been bribed. When he raised the heavy grill to let Mrs. Young go down to her husband, twenty-eight prisoners rushed up, overpowered and wounded the unbribed guard, and made their escape. Often escapees from the mine were quickly picked up and brought back, but these twenty-eight men had planned well, and most got clean away.

Jonathan Trumbull became deputy governor when William Pitkin succeeded Thomas Fitch as governor in 1766. In 1769 Governor Pitkin died and Trumbull took his place, remaining at this post until 1784. He was the only governor to declare openly for the colonial cause when war broke out.

In all, more than half of the prisoners who were confined at Simsbury during the Revolution escaped. After one last fire, in November 1782, Newgate was closed and not reopened until long afterward.

Jonathan Trumbull

Before becoming Connecticut's war governor, Jonathan Trumbull had an illustrious career as a member of the General Assembly and as deputy governor. Becoming governor in 1769 upon the death of William Pitkin, he was, in fact, the only governor of a colony who was not an appointee of the king or a Loyalist at the outbreak of the Revolution and who remained in office throughout the conflict.

Jonathan Trumbull grew to maturity in the town of Lebanon in eastern Connecticut. Lebanon in those years was just emerging from its frontier stage of development, and Joseph Trumbull, Jonathan's father, was active in both local affairs and in the business of trading local livestock in Boston for English manufactured goods.

Born in 1710, Jonathan went to Harvard, where his father expected him to become a Congregational minister. His years at Harvard, however, were uneventful, although the young Jonathan became thoroughly indoctrinated in Puritan thought and practice.

When his older brother died at sea in 1731, Jonathan was asked to help his father in the family business. This was a turning point in his life. In time he became an important inland merchant, one who relied on coastal merchants for the sale of the goods he had to sell in exchange for manufactured goods from abroad. His liberal credit policy toward his friends and neighbors brought him to the verge of bankruptcy several times as creditors in Boston, New York, and London demanded payment. Trumbull was able, however, to use his political offices of deputy governor and governor to forestall his creditors.

In spite of Trumbull's humiliating experiences in business in the years prior to the Revolutionary War, he emerged from the war as "one of the major contributors to the American victory." From the beginning of the war at Lexington and Concord, Trumbull was at the center of the war effort. He more than anyone else was responsible for the mobilization of Connecticut's physical and economic resources, and he made sure that vital supplies went to Washington and the Continental Army. At the urging of Trumbull, Connecticut's citizens not only took care of their own troops but on numerous occasions sent herds of cattle to the starving troops at Valley Forge and Morristown.

Washington soon came to rely on the Connecticut governor. When there was a shortage of supplies in the Continental Army, as happened often enough, he would say to his staff, "We must consult Brother Jonathan."

From this oft-used comment, the term "Brother Jonathan" came to be synonymous with "Yankee." To Southerners it meant a New Englander. To foreigners it meant an American.

As the Continental currency decreased in value, the Connecticut farmers became more reluctant to sell their products. However, when the French forces came to Newport, Rhode Island, and offered gold for the grain and cattle, the supplies flowed freely to Rochambeau's troops.

Trumbull was also responsible for seeing that two other essential elements of warfare, gunpowder and guns, were supplied to the American troops. At the beginning of the conflict over 90 percent of the gunpowder came from Europe, but soon Connecticut had mills producing powder at East Hartford, Windham, New Haven, Stratford, Glastonbury, and Salisbury. The production was limited, however, by the scarcity of saltpeter and sulfur. The manufacture of guns increased as a bounty of five shillings per gun was offered to the skilled craftsman in gunmaking. The gunsmiths in Goshen, Mansfield, and Windham supplied enough weapons so that all Connecticut soldiers joining the Continental Army were armed.

Governor Trumbull and the General Assembly took control of the iron foundries in Salisbury. These foundries produced cannon, grapeshot, and round shot that went mainly to arm the coastal towns, which feared raids by the British on inland supply depots—and with good reason, as we shall see.

The governor wasn't the only member of the Trumbull family to make his name in the war. Son Jonathan joined the army and served, with the rank of colonel, on Washington's staff. Son Joseph served in the Continental Congress, on the board of war, and as commissary general to the army. Son John, the youngest, was an artist and created a classic series of paintings of the war's high points, many now on display in the Capitol in Washington.

CHAPTER TEN

Connecticut Men at War

In spite of the American victories at Trenton and Princeton, around Christmas 1776, the British in the spring of 1777 were confident the end of the conflict was near. General Clinton had taken Newport, Rhode Island, and planned to subdue New England. General Burgoyne expected to move south from Canada through the Hudson Valley, thereby splitting the rebelling colonies in two. Washington was not sure whether General Howe, in control of New York, would move up the Hudson to join Burgoyne or south to Philadelphia or possibly Charleston.

Since the days of the Stamp Act, western Connecticut had been an area sympathetic to the Loyalist cause. So when word was received early in April that a "large magazine of military stores and provisions" had been collected at Danbury, Howe decided to move quickly in order to destroy the mounting criticism that he was an inactive general. An expedition into Connecticut would serve therefore not only as a diversionary move but would also deprive the American forces in the lower Hudson area of much-needed supplies. Because Danbury was located in western Connecticut, very little opposition was expected from the local Tory inhabitants.

When Howe moved south, he left some four thousand troops in New York under the command of the royal governor, William Tryon. Finding his civil responsibilities as governor dull after a distinguished career in the British army, Tryon applied for active duty and was commissioned a major general of the Provincials. Under orders from Howe to attack Danbury and destroy the military supplies there, on the afternoon of April 25, Tryon landed at the mouth of the Saugatuck River with a force of about two thousand. They marched inland and spent the night in Weston.

The appearance of so many British soldiers sent Patriot messengers in all directions to spread the alarm. Benedict Arnold, "sulking at his sister's home and itching for a fight," hurried over from New Haven and joined the militia, which was gathering from all over Fairfield County.

Tryon's troops marched to Danbury virtually unopposed. Upon arriving in Danbury, the British began a methodical destruction of all the supplies. Only a few medical supplies were successfully removed by the Americans before the British arrival. Although Tryon gave orders to destroy the rum, hundreds of his men became gloriously drunk as they set fire to houses and barns. As darkness fell, Tryon realized that he was in a precarious position with a majority of his men helplessly intoxicated and an undetermined number of militia closing in on him. The order to evacuate was given, but before they left, Danbury was virtually destroyed.

Joseph Plumb Martin, participating in the defense, had an ample opportunity to see the destruction caused by the British. He reported that "the town had been laid in ashes, a number of the inhabitants murdered and cast into their burning houses, because they presumed to defend their persons and property, or to be avenged on a cruel, vindictive invading enemy." Martin felt that the British had "fully executed their design."

As the British withdrew, the American militia began their harassing tactics of shooting from behind stone walls, trees, and buildings. Before the British got back to their ships, their losses were close to two hundred while the Americans had only twenty killed and forty wounded. General Wooster, who had been placed in command of the militia, was among those fatally wounded. Benedict Arnold had two horses shot out from under him, but he miraculously escaped each time.

The final chapter in Israel Putnam's legendary career occurred in the countryside near Redding, when he escaped General Tryon's troops by riding on horseback down a long flight of stone steps at Horseneck in the town of Greenwich. Soon after that feat, while he was in command of troops on the west side of the Hudson, his military career came to an end when he suffered a stroke and became paralyzed.

Disaster at Forty Fort

No Connecticut men suffered more than those who had moved south and west to settle in Pennsylvania's Wyoming Valley (near modern Wilkes-Barre). Here in this fertile region along the east branch of the Susquehanna River, about twenty-five miles long, lived a flourishing population of some five thousand people. Pennsylvania had not welcomed these Yankee newcomers and, of course, did not recognize Connecticut's claim of jurisdiction over them. There had been several pitched battles between them and Pennsylvania authorities before the Quaker colony gave up and let them stay. So, although they continued to occupy the farms and settlements of the region, Pennsylvania felt no obligation to protect the Wyoming Valley people, and when the Revolution broke out, the young men of the valley enlisted in Connecticut's forces. The entire community was isolated and weak.

There were a number of small forts and fortified houses in the valley, the chief of which was called Forty Fort, after the number of emigrants in the first party to settle there. When, on June 30, 1778, a force of Tory rangers appeared in the valley, settlers fled to these various strongpoints and barricaded themselves in. The rangers were under the command of Colonel John Butler, a grim, able, and wrathful New Yorker who had been hounded off his own lands because of his Loyalist leanings. He set off down the Wyoming Valley and for the next few days made prisoners of those settlers who surrendered and burned out those who didn't. Finally, on July 3, he reached Forty Fort, where the major portion of the local militia was holed up, under the command of a Continental officer, Colonel Zebulon Butler (no relation to John). The Patriot Butler decided to go out and meet the Loyalist Butler in open battle.

At first all seemed to go well with the Wyoming militia. The invading Tories allowed themselves to be stopped, then pushed back in what looked like a retreat. At length, taking refuge behind a previously prepared breastwork, the Tories faced about, and in that moment, a hidden force of Indians leaped up from their hiding places on either side. It was an ambush.

The militia broke and fled, and the Indians and Tories went after them. Some plunged into the nearby Susquehanna, in hopes of escaping to the other banks, but the Indians were better swimmers than they and more lightly clothed, and soon the beautiful river was choked with corpses. It was one of the most devastating Loyalist victories of the entire war, and it was a long time before the region recovered from the blow.

The following day, however, when Forty Fort itself surrendered, the men, women, and children within it were allowed to depart unharmed. And although the episode has gone down in history as the Wyoming Massacre, it is fairer to consider it as simply a defeat for the American cause.

More British Raids

The following winter, General Tryon was back in Connecticut. On February 29, 1779, he led an invasion assault against Greenwich in an attempt to destroy the saltworks in the area. This brief raid was successful in that the saltworks were destroyed, there was wide pillaging, and many livestock were captured.

Later that year in July, on the third anniversary of the Declaration of Independence, British troops landed in the New Haven area, and "what was to be a day of joy developed into a day of tragedy and horror." General Garth's troops debarked at West Haven. Led by a Tory Yale student, they were intercepted by Yale's elderly and passionately Patriotic ex-president Naphtali Daggert on his old black mare. Daggert's legendary action, which resulted in his being wounded and captured by the British, was not lost on the Yale students and townspeople participating in the defense of New Haven. A Yale senior later described the incident:

> I well remember the surprise we felt as we were marching over West Bridge toward the enemy, to see Dr. Daggert riding furiously by us on his old black mare, with his long fowling piece in his hand, ready for action. We knew the old gentleman had studied the matter thoroughly, and settled his own mind as to the right and propriety of fighting it out, but were not quite prepared to see him come forth in so gallant a style to carry his principles into practice.

Aaron Burr, visiting relatives in his former hometown, volunteered his services and led a small group of militia. General Tryon's forces invading from the east sent out a number of raiding parties and met greater resistance than did Garth's. The British stayed in New Haven only a day,

New Haven during the War of the Revolution.

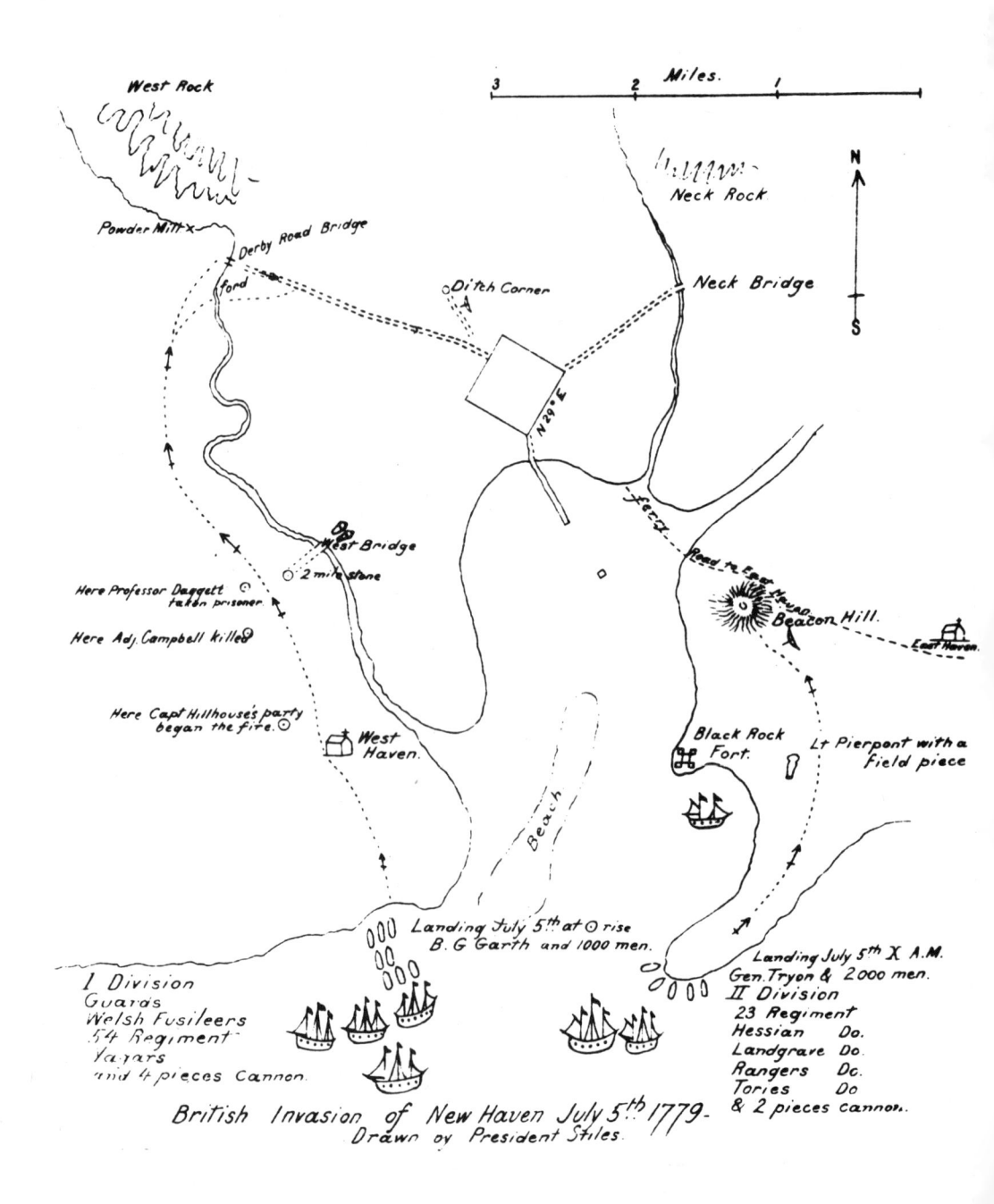

British Invasion of New Haven July 5th 1779.
Drawn by President Stiles.

during which time they pillaged the town and got "dreadfully drunk" on confiscated rum.

Yale President Ezra Stiles recorded in his diary: "From the first Entrance till VIII in the Eveng. the [town] was given up to Ravage and Plunder, from which only a few Houses were protected." While the British looted at random and destroyed many household furnishings, the town "fared much better than we feared, as we expected nothing but to see the town reduced to ashes." Since Yale College was the largest university in America at this time and a hotbed of rebellion, it is strange that the British did not destroy it and the town. Tradition has it that New Haven Loyalists persuaded the British not to destroy the churches, public buildings, and the college. Before the British left, however, the commander invited the Tory families to accompany his troops, but only four families joined them.

On their return to New York the British put the torch to the towns of Fairfield and Norwalk. Although these towns were almost completely destroyed, there were very few casualties on either side.

The most brutal attack on any Connecticut town came in the final year of the war when Benedict Arnold, who by then had joined the British, led an attack against New London, a leading shipping and privateering center. Arnold planned to enter the harbor and destroy the military supplies and shipping before the militia had time to rally. He had grown up in the region and knew the area well.

Benedict Arnold

Benedict Arnold was born in Norwich on January 14, 1741. His family was well known and respected, and his mother was "austere, pious and domineering." Arnold's father, however, who was considered a ne'er-do-well, died in poverty and drunkenness. As a youth Arnold was rebellious and showed an unconventional attitude toward life. At fourteen he ran away from home after being apprenticed to a druggist. He saw military service in the French and Indian War, but when the glamour of the war

---

The invasion of New Haven by the British on the third anniversary of the signing of the Declaration of Independence was taken as a personal insult by President Ezra Stiles of Yale.

Benedict Arnold, the notorious traitor, eventually led an attack by the British against his former neighbors in New London.

diminished and homesickness set in, he deserted. Only his youth saved him from serious punishment.

At twenty-one he set himself up as a druggist and bookseller in New Haven. His business prospered, and he also entered into the more profitable sideline of selling horses and mules to planters in the West Indies. In 1767 he married Margaret Mansfield of New Haven and had three sons. His business successes marked him as a citizen of consequence in New Haven, and he became captain of one of the town's militia companies.

When the Revolutionary War began, Arnold's company was among the first to join the fighting in Boston. Later he and Ethan Allen of the Green Mountain Boys led the attack on Fort Ticonderoga in May 1775, in order to capture the military supplies known to be stored there. Not willing to share glory or credit, Arnold soon was quarreling with Allen, another of the same stripe. He led a separate expedition to the northern end of Lake Champlain, where he captured the fort at St. John's and destroyed the post and its supplies.

When he returned to Cambridge, he was accused of mishandling funds entrusted to him for the expedition. The leader of the investigating committee was, ironically, Dr. Benjamin Church of Boston, who later was also discovered to be a traitor to the American cause. Arnold, however, was cleared of the charges when it became known that he had actually used his own personal credit to finance the expedition. The Continental Congress later voted to reimburse him.

During the summer of 1775 Arnold proposed another expedition against Canada. Washington was receptive to the idea, and so in September Arnold and his men left for the Kennebec River in Maine, where two hundred river boats were waiting for them. In an epic six-week journey up turbulent, cataract-ridden streams, through wintry forests, and across snowy swamps, Arnold led his men to the gates of Quebec. There he joined forces with Brigadier General Richard Montgomery, who had recently seized Montreal, and the pair launched a two-pronged assault on the Canadian capitol.

The ill-fated attack was launched on a night of wild wind and snow. Montgomery was slain almost immediately, whereupon his men retreated in haste. For his part, Arnold was wounded in the right knee and turned over command to his burly subordinate, Virginian Daniel Morgan. Morgan, a towering figure, managed to penetrate deep into Quebec's Lower Town, but few of Arnold's men followed him, and soon the British defenders rallied and surrounded him. The attack failed, Morgan became a British prisoner, and Arnold was forced to make a disastrous retreat in the spring.

Thus the campaign failed in its original objective, but the memorable offensive inspired many of Arnold's countrymen to emulate him. His courage and endurance in leading his men on so grueling an expedition, his brilliance in conceiving such an enterprising strategy at all, and his example in attacking a fortress city against great odds—these things made men remember the name "Benedict Arnold."

The British then devised a plan whereby they expected to cut off New England from the rest of the colonies by gaining control of the Hudson Valley and Lake Champlain. Once that was done, London strategists felt, New England, the "heart" of the rebellion, could be easily subdued, and the remaining colonies would be glad to abandon the struggle.

Arnold forestalled this scheme by engaging General Sir Guy Carleton in two naval battles off Valcour Island (in Lake Champlain) and Crown Point in October 1776. The British were ultimately victorious, but the battles so delayed their invasion that it was put off a full year.

In 1777 a full-scale expedition was launched from Canada down the Champlain–Hudson line. Its commander, Lieutenant General John Burgoyne, easily took Fort Ticonderoga and sailed out onto the lower reaches of Lake Champlain and Lake George. Between there and the navigable part of the Hudson, however, was a "land bridge"—twenty miles of upland forest, through which he had to build a road and over which he had to hump supplies, before he could continue his invasion. Here American troops, under the direction of Major General Philip Schuyler, dammed streams, logged trees across the road, broke down bridges, and generally delayed the expedition for so long that it was mid-September before Burgoyne had crossed the Hudson and started for Albany, his objective.

In the meantime, Arnold had been sent to relieve Fort Schuyler (modern Rome, New York), which was under siege by a combined force of British, Indians, and Tories. An earlier attempt to relieve it by a unit of New York militia had ended in the bloody battle of Oriskany, and although the Indians had turned back the relief force, they were disgruntled at having had to do most of the fighting. Arnold learned of this. Fearing that his own troops could not march fast enough to reach the beleaguered fort in time, he employed a stratagem: Releasing a simpleminded Tory prisoner, he sent him ahead to spread the word among the Indians that an enormous force of Americans was about to descend upon them, as numerous as the leaves of the trees. It worked. The Indians abandoned the siege, and the British and Tories were forced to retreat.

On his return from this assignment, Arnold rejoined the American main force, now under a new commander, Major General Horatio Gates, a fussy, uninspired leader. The Americans held a strongly fortified position on a ridge overlooking the Hudson, and their guns barred the British from using the river route. On September 19, Burgoyne attempted to bypass Gates by swinging around the Americans' left.

Arnold was the first to perceive what the British were up to. He urged the apathetic Gates to move out and stop them, but Gates did not want to leave his secure fortifications. At length, however, he gave his subordinate permission to lead out some riflemen and light infantry to see what they could do. The subsequent clash is known as the first battle of Saratoga.

Arnold was everywhere, stopping the British right wing, slicing between it and the center, calling for reinforcements to press home the attack. Long afterward an eyewitness recalled that day:

> Nothing could exceed the bravery of Arnold on this day; he seemed the very genius of war. Infuriated by the conflict and maddened by Gates' refusal to send reinforcements, which he repeatedly called for, and knowing he was meeting the brunt of the battle, he seemed inspired with the fury of a demon.

A long, hard day of fighting ended in a stalemate. The British hadn't advanced; the Americans hadn't stopped them. For three weeks the two armies faced each other, the British occupying themselves in building several strong redoubts, or field fortifications, the Americans being reinforced until they outnumbered their opponents overwhelmingly. Then, on October 7, Burgoyne renewed the attack.

Arnold, who had received no credit from Gates for his valiant part in the September 19 scrap, had been confined to quarters for quarreling with his superior. When he heard the guns on October 7, he forgot about orders, mounted his horse, and headed straight for the smell of gunpowder.

Gates had already organized a counterattack against the advancing British. Arnold put himself at the head of it and pressed the assault so furiously that there was a general British fallback all along the line. Not content, Arnold pursued them into one redoubt, and when that proved too strong for his men, he switched about and assaulted another. That one fell, and almost the last shot its defenders fired wounded Arnold in the leg—the same limb injured at Quebec.

By the following night, Burgoyne was in retreat, and nine days later, on October 17, he surrendered at the little town of Saratoga. It was to be the turning point of the war.

Despite the enmity of Gates, Arnold was widely acclaimed the hero of the two battles. Returning to Connecticut to recuperate from his wound, he was warmly received by the people. Nevertheless, it was several months before he was directed by General Washington to take command of Philadelphia, from which the British had withdrawn.

Philadelphia, the City of Brotherly Love, proved to be the downfall of Arnold. Caught up in the social life of the city, the largest and most sophisticated in the colonies, he lived beyond his means, piling up debts.

There also, he met the nineteen-year-old Peggy Shippen, "the darling of Philadelphia society." Arnold, whose wife had died in 1775, found Peggy irresistible, and they were married in April 1779.

Peggy's Tory sympathies and Arnold's Puritan background caused him to resent the alliance with Catholic France, which his victory at Saratoga had brought about. Furthermore, the proud, high-spirited Norwich man could not get along equably with his fellow officers and with members of the Continental Congress, and this contributed to his disillusion. Secretly he began to feed military information to the British.

Washington, unaware of Arnold's deep involvement in treason, continued to have faith in him and tried to place him in an active command. Instead, Arnold insisted on the command of West Point, a strategic military position in the central Hudson Valley, covered by a series of forts and gun emplacements. Possession of West Point, which guarded the New York Highlands, blocked passage of Royal Navy vessels to the upper river, and protected the army's main routes of supply between New England and New Jersey, was absolutely vital to the American cause. Arnold agreed to betray it for £20,000.

The person with whom he carried on his treasonous correspondence was Major John André, adjutant general of the British Army, an old friend of Peggy, and a man of great charm and popularity. (Even the Americans like André.) On September 21, 1780, he journeyed up the Hudson in a naval vessel to meet and finalize plans with Arnold, meaning to return by the same vessel the next day. Instead, the vessel was forced by American artillery to move downriver, and André had to make his way back by horseback. At Tarrytown, New York, he was seized, identified as a spy, and turned over to Washington. By September 25, the plot—and Arnold's share in it—was revealed. Arnold escaped to the British, and Washington was left with only André, who was hanged as a spy.

The British had not gotten what they really wanted from Benedict Arnold, but they commissioned him a brigadier general of Provincial (Tory) troops. After some action in Virginia, in which Richmond was burned, Arnold was directed by Sir Henry Clinton to lead a raid on New London.

New London lies on the west bank of the Thames River, Groton on the east, and each community was protected by a fort. On September 6,

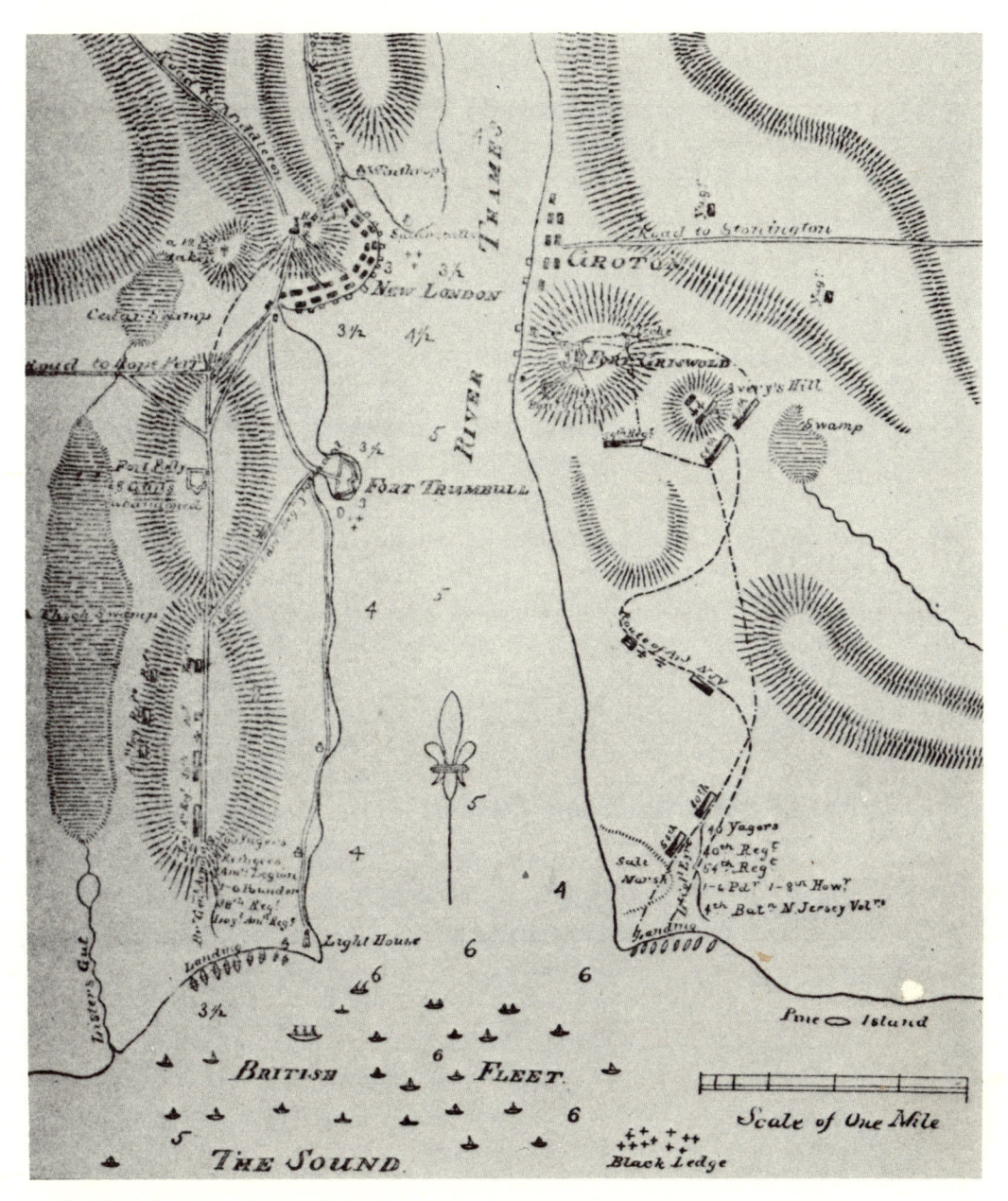

New London was destroyed by fire, and the troops at Groton were massacred in the attack by the British on September 6, 1781.

1781, Arnold landed his forces in two divisions. One, under Lieutenant Colonel Edmund Eyre, was sent against Fort Griswold (Groton), and he himself led the other against Fort Trumbull (New London). Arnold burned the shipping and most of the town, then advanced against the fort, which was hastily evacuated. But Fort Griswold, under the command of Lieutenant Colonel William Ledyard, fended off three separate attacks, making in Arnold's own words "a most obstinate defense of near forty minutes."

The assaulting force heavily outnumbered the defenders, however, and on the fourth attack, British and Tory troops came pouring into the fort. Colonel Ledyard, having no choice but to surrender, held out his sword, hilt first. A Tory officer seized the weapon and ran it back through Ledyard's body—the senseless murder of an unarmed man. As though that were a signal, the king's troops proceeded to bayonet the rest of the surrendered garrison.

The Fort Griswold massacre was hardly Arnold's personal fault, but his bland glossing over of the facts in his official report—"Eighty-five men were found dead in Fort Griswold, and 60 wounded, most of them mortally"—and his wanton destruction of a town that lay only a dozen miles from his birthplace finished off his already infamous reputation. Benedict Arnold was to be his country's greatest villain.

Washington Also Slept Here

George Washington passed through New Haven, Hartford, and Springfield in June 1775 on his way to Cambridge, where he took command of the colonial forces. Washington's selection as commander in chief, initiated by John Adams of Massachusetts, was a compromise gesture in order to unite the colonies in the war effort. The *Courant* in Hartford had only a brief notice on July 3 of both Washington's appointment and his journey to Cambridge to assume command. It did note, however, the following April that "the Lady of his Excellency General WASHINGTON, passed through this Town, on her Way to New-York."

Washington's most important visits to Connecticut during the war occurred in 1780 and 1781. As a result of the victory at Saratoga, France entered the war on the side of the Americans. The first French troops landed at Newport on July 11, 1780, under the command of General Jean Baptiste Donatien, Comte de Rochambeau, and a meeting between Rochambeau and Washington was arranged by Lafayette at the Wadsworth home in Hartford. Governor Trumbull attended the meeting where "the greatest satisfaction was expressed by the parties . . . and the highest marks of polite respect and attention were mutual." Washington returned to West Point after this meeting just too late to prevent Benedict Arnold, his treachery revealed, from escaping to the British.

The following March Washington returned again to Connecticut on his way to Newport for a second conference with the French. A third conference was held in May 1781, and Washington recorded in his diary for the nineteenth: "Breakfasted at Litchfield—dined at Farmington—and lodged at Wethersfield at the house of Joseph Webb. . . ." The house, an excellent example of eighteenth-century New England Georgian architecture, was filled with exquisite furnishings, and the lady of the house, famed as a hostess, had Washington's room papered with expensive French wall covering in preparation for his visit.

The following day Washington "had a good deal of private conversation with Govr. Trumbull," and consulted with Colonel Jeremiah Wadsworth and others about Connecticut's cooperation in the final phases of the war. The value of the Continental paper currency had declined greatly, and as a result Wadsworth and others had preferred sending quantities of food and supplies to the French for hard money, so that Washington's troops had suffered. This was no doubt the subject of much of the conversation. At this meeting, which lasted five days at the Webb house, Washington and Rochambeau devised the plans that ultimately led to the Yorktown victory.

CHAPTER ELEVEN

The Constitution State Joins the Union

Lord Cornwallis surrendered his army of almost eight thousand men to Washington on October 19, 1781, and the American independence was ensured. Governor Trumbull received word of the victory on October 26 and rejoiced along with the rest of the state.

The news of Yorktown indicated that the end of the fighting was at hand. The United States still maintained its army, but no more battles were fought. Diplomatic negotiations began, and the preliminary articles of peace were signed on November 30, 1782. The news of the formal British acknowledgment of our independence reached Connecticut in April 1783.

New Haven and Yale College celebrated the news on Thursday, April 24, by beginning their ceremonies at dawn with the firing of thirteen cannon on the green. At nine o'clock "Congress's Proclamation for the Cessation of Hostilities" was read to a packed meetinghouse. This was followed by a forty-minute prayer of thanksgiving by President Stiles of Yale and a thirty-minute oration by one of the tutors. These services began and ended with the singing of anthems.

A public dinner was followed in the afternoon by another thirteen-cannon salute to the United States at three o'clock, a twenty-one gun salute to France and Spain at four, and a seven-gun salute to Holland at five. (Holland and Spain had entered the war against Britain as France's ally, but not America's.) Fireworks and a bonfire finished the evening. Although liquor was available, "there was little, very little Excess and in general great Decorum. An almost universal Joy and Congratulation diffused itself among all." After the bonfire burned down, the crowd gave three rousing cheers and then "all broke up and retired peacefully home."

Hartford held its celebration on April 30, but its fireworks set the local courthouse on fire.

In May the General Assembly repealed nearly all the wartime economic and military laws even though the definitive Peace of Paris was not actually signed until September 3, 1783.

Postwar Issues

In spite of its modest population of 200,000, Connecticut's total manpower contribution to the war effort was very large. Close to 40,000 men saw military service of some kind, although many of the enlistments were for a short duration. The issue of veterans' benefits and pensions was hotly debated after Congress granted five years full pay to the Continental Army officers. In many towns this was unpopular, and several town meetings declared the act "unwise, unjust, and illegal," since the enlisted men and the militia, both officers and men, were left out altogether. There was considerable opposition also to the formation of the Society of Cincinnati, an organization of former Continental Army officers. The General Assembly finally followed the lead of the Confederation Acts of 1786 and 1788 and awarded benefits to all who were disabled in the service. This veterans' issue, which set military rank against rank, did much to prepare the way for the future Jeffersonian party in Connecticut.

The number of Loyalists was relatively small in proportion to the population and largely confined to the southwestern part of the state. It has been stated that Connecticut's "attitude toward the Loyalists was firm and decided, it was not vindictive or revengeful." As a result there was not a general spirit of resentment after the war, but rather an attempt of reconciliation with the remaining Loyalists as they became part of the new economic conservatism of the postwar period.

Connecticut continued with many regional differences, but the postwar period brought up new problems that were statewide. Their experiences in the war caused many citizens to take a whole new outlook on life, especially those who had traveled far from home for the first time. As after all wars, the returned veteran was not content with conditions in the Land of Steady Habits. The wartime inflation made much of the currency practically worthless, and the expression "not worth a Continental" entered the language.

Connecticut was faced with the choice of action of returning to her semi-isolationism and quasi-economic independence or of adhering to the new concept of "the confederated welfare of the United States." The economic forces at work, however, favored the more vigorous national point of view. These forces soon made themselves felt not only in the economic and political areas but also in social life and religion.

A law passed in 1784 prevented any members of the legislature and executive branches of state government or members of Congress from serving on the Superior Court. The General Assembly also created a new Supreme Court of Errors as the highest and final court of appeals from the Superior Court.

The Quakers in Rhode Island were the first group in New England to protest against slavery as a moral issue. In 1758 they forbade their members to purchase slaves or to engage in the slave trade, and by the time of the Revolution slave ownership among them was no longer permitted. The freeing of slaves in Connecticut was greatly accelerated by the Revolution through the use of slaves as substitutes for white men in the Continental Army. With the coming of peace the antislavery sentiment was legislated into action. In 1784 an act was passed that no Negro or mulatto born in Connecticut after March 1 should be held a slave after reaching the age of twenty-five. There is no exact information on the number of adult slaves who were freed, but the fact is known that slavery was no longer profitable. The actual number of slaves in the state steadily decreased after 1774, until the first United States census, in 1790, showed more free Negroes than slaves: 2,759 slaves against 2,801 free Negroes.

The Anglican or Episcopal clergy, who had espoused the Patriot cause during the Revolution, once more began to take an active part in community life. Even though the Congregational Church was to remain "the established church" until 1818, fourteen Episcopal clergymen met in Woodbury in March 1783 to select Samuel Seabury, one of their members, to go to England to seek consecration as a bishop. Because he was unable to swear an oath of supremacy to the British sovereign, Seabury went to

Scotland and was consecrated by the "nonjuring" bishops of Scotland. Returning in the spring of 1785, he preached as the first Episcopal bishop in the United States of America in his father's old parish in New London. He later joined with clergy from the southern states, where the Church of England had been the prevailing church, in establishing the Protestant Episcopal Church in the United States, at a convention held in Philadelphia in October 1789.

Migrations from Connecticut

Considering the prevailing agricultural practices and the serious soil depletion on many marginal farmlands, postwar Connecticut was fast approaching a population saturation point. It was perhaps the most densely populated among the thirteen states. In spite of an exodus that began about the middle of the century and gained momentum after the final defeat of the French in 1760, the state's population continued to increase. The first United States census in 1790 put the population at 237,946. This was a gain of 29,076 since the end of the war in 1782.

The availability of cheap and fertile land on the frontiers was appealing to everyone. An area to receive many Connecticut settlers was western Massachusetts. The towns of Pittsfield, Stockbridge, and Williamstown were in the beginning virtually Connecticut towns, and soon the Connecticut influence spread to the rest of Berkshire County. Land hunger and land speculation were the chief reasons for the settling of Vermont. Many of the names of Vermont towns reflect the origins of their original settlers. Other reasons for the migration to Vermont were the economic distress caused by the inflation during the Revolution, the marginal or submarginal quality of land in towns like Barkhamsted and Colebrook, and a desire to escape the religious and political restrictions of the old Connecticut towns.

In 1788 Rufus Putnam, a cousin of Israel, led a group of New Englanders to the confluence of the Muskingum and Ohio rivers, to establish the first settlement in what would later become the State of Ohio. Feeling that Americans owed a great debt to the French king and queen for their help in winning the Revolution, they named their town for Marie Antoinette: Marietta.

Many other towns in New York State, Pennsylvania, Ohio, and points west were settled by migrants from Connecticut, who took with them the cherished institutions of old Connecticut—the Congregational Church, the town meeting, the village school, the respect for higher education, and rugged individualism. This migration continued well into the twentieth century. In fact, some towns in the rural eastern and western parts of Connecticut did not gain back their Revolutionary populations until after World War II.

Roger Sherman

No one contributed more or brought more honor to Connecticut during the last quarter of the eighteenth century than Roger Sherman. He was "the one man in America who had helped shape and who had signed every great document of the war and independence, of peace and government, from the first days of the First Continental Congress." He is the only man who had the unique honor of signing the Association of 1774 establishing the intercolonial boycott of British goods, the Declaration of Rights of 1774, the Declaration of Independence, the Articles of Confederation, the Peace of Paris of 1783, and the Federal Constitution of 1787. No other man put his name to even four of these six documents.

Roger Sherman began life as the son of a humble shoemaker, and his father taught him the shoemaker's trade. After the death of his father, Sherman at the age of twenty became the main support of his mother and the younger children. In 1754 he began the practice of law, and after the death of his wife in 1760, he moved his family from New Milford to New Haven, where he went into the mercantile business. Appointed treasurer of Yale College in 1765, he held that post until other duties interfered. He also became active in local and state affairs as a judge of the county court and as a member of the upper house of the General Assembly.

Elected a delegate to the First Continental Congress in 1774, he was in continual attendance at the Congress for the next eight years, as long as the war lasted. One of its most influential members, he served on many committees and was known for his capacity for hard work and his blunt and honest speech. Wrote a modern admirer of Roger Sherman:

Samuel Huntington, one of the signers of the Declaration of Independence, was governor when Connecticut ratified the United States Constitution.

He had a grasp of broad principles without the slightest pedantry; he was firm in his moral beliefs yet not dogmatic or intolerant; he knew law well, without being legalistic; he stuck to his guns staunchly but avoided arguments and never shirked reasonable compromise.

Furthermore, "he won men to reason and moderation by his calmness, knowledge, and sense of justice. . . ."

The Federal Constitution

As some postwar problems came to be resolved, others persisted. Hard times and frequent foreclosures for debt drove Massachusetts farmers to the rising known as Shays's Rebellion. Settlers in the Connecticut Valley and the Berkshire Hills armed themselves and forcibly prevented the courts from sitting, so that debt collection could not be ordered. Troops restored order, but the insurgents were all hastily pardoned, for there was much public sympathy on their side.

In many other parts of the new United States, men were growing more and more dissatisfied with the ineffectiveness of their national government. This led to a call for the Philadelphia Convention of 1787 to revise the Articles of Confederation.

Governor Samuel Huntington, a former president of the Continental Congress and a signer of the Declaration of Independence, favored Connecticut's participation, and after vigorous debate in the General Assembly, the supporters of revision were successful. The assembly chose Roger Sherman, Oliver Ellsworth, and William Samuel Johnson as delegates.

Oliver Ellsworth, the youngest of the three, was respected as one of the leading lawyers in the state. He had served six years in the Continental Congress, where his administrative ability was recognized. In 1785 he was appointed a judge of the Superior Court. After the ratification of the Federal Constitution, he was one of Connecticut's first two Senators and was appointed in 1796 as Chief Justice of the Supreme Court of the United States.

William Samuel Johnson was unique among the Revolutionary leaders of Connecticut in that he was raised an Anglican. He was graduated from Yale in 1744, got a master's degree from Harvard in 1747, and in 1766 was granted the degree of doctor of civil laws by Oxford University. Opposed to the Stamp Act, he was one of three Connecticut delegates to the Stamp Act Congress in New York, but as a conservative he never favored the violent tactics of the Sons of Liberty. He opposed the separation from England and was debarred from legal practice for failure to take an oath of allegiance to the "free and independent" State of Connecticut. After 1776 he retired to his home in Stratford and refused to support a war either against his neighbors or against the Crown. He eventually resumed his law practice and after the war became a member of the General Assembly. From 1787 to 1800 he was president of Columbia College in New York, and until 1791, when the national capital moved to Philadelphia, he was the other United States Senator from Connecticut.

The three delegates, although representing different shades of opinion, were in harmony with each other. They took an active part in the deliberations at the Constitutional Convention in Philadelphia. Their most important contribution was the famous Connecticut Compromise. The original proposal was "that the proportion of suffrage in the first branch should be according to the respective numbers of free inhabitants, and that in the second branch or Senate each state should have one vote and no more." This was finally modified to allow two Senators from each state, but representation in the House of Representatives was to be based on the state's population.

Ratification Completed

Upon their return home all three delegates enthusiastically endorsed the new Constitution. On October 1, 1787, the *Courant* printed the long-awaited text of the proposed Constitution of the United States of America. Ellsworth, writing in plain, clear language, had thirteen letters printed in the *Courant* between November 5, 1787, and March 24, 1788. He aimed his arguments primarily at the farmers and stressed that "the prosperity and riches of the farmer must depend on the prosperity, and good national regulation of trade." Roger Sherman also had five letters in other newspapers in which he stressed the importance of a strong central government. At this time the *Courant* claimed a circulation of about 8,000 subscribers. Consequently, these letters and the *Courant's* enthusiastic backing of the need for a stronger union of the states did much to stimulate public interest in the document.

The leaders supporting the new Constitution were men who saw the advantages of a strong central government. Practically all of them were lawyers or merchants and in some cases both. The advantages of free trade on a national scale appealed to them. They were men from the larger towns and experienced in the workings of government. Most of them had served in the Continental Congress and knew first hand the advantages and need for interstate cooperation. Furthermore, these Federalists were extremely articulate.

The opposition, on the other hand, represented the more rural areas of the state. The anti-Federalists disliked the large increase in power granted the national government, especially the provisions for laying duties on imports and the financial and military powers. The memory of the failure of Shays's Rebellion in Massachusetts was still with many of them. They lacked lines of communication, and no Connecticut newspaper would publish their compositions.

In October 1787 the General Assembly voted unanimously to call a special convention for the consideration of the Constitution. Elected in November, the delegates convened on January 4, 1788, in Hartford. The convention met at the State House but was driven by the cold weather to the First Society Meeting House, which was heated. No vote was taken until the Constitution was read in full and each section thoroughly debated. The public filled the galleries. The *Courant's* editors followed the debates closely and allowed the news of Connecticut's ratification of the Constitution to push other items off the pages. They realized these were historic times and "if the advertisers didn't like it, they could console themselves with the crisp notice: 'Advertisements, &c., omitted for want of room, will appear in our next.'"

Ellsworth and Johnson opened the debates and strongly defended the document. Governor Huntington and Lieutenant Governor Oliver Wolcott also supported ratification. The *Courant,* sensing the greatness of the occasion, quoted Governor Huntington:

> This is a new event in the history of mankind.—Heretofore, most governments have been formed by tyrants, and imposed on mankind by force. Never before did a people, in time of peace and tranquility, meet together by their representatives, and with calm deliberation frame for themselves a system of government. . . .

In answer to the fear that the central government might become too strong, Huntington replied, "There is at present an extreme want of power in the national government; it is my opinion that this constitution does not give too much."

After five days of prolonged debate the vote on January 9, 1788, showed only forty opposing ratification whereas 128 approved. With such forceful backing, Connecticut, the original Constitution State, became the fifth state in the union to ratify the new Federal Constitution.

Important Dates

1614	Adriaen Block, representing the Dutch, sails up the Connecticut River.
1633	The Dutch erect a fort, the House of (Good) Hope, on the present site of Hartford. John Oldham and others explore and trade along the Connecticut River. Plymouth Colony sends William Holmes to found a trading post at Windsor.
1634	Wethersfield founded by people from Watertown, Massachusetts.
1635	Fort erected at Saybrook by Lion Gardiner. Group from Dorchester, Massachusetts, joins Windsor settlement, and people from New Town, Massachusetts, found Hartford.
1636	Thomas Hooker and company journey from New Town (Cambridge), Massachusetts, to settle at Hartford.
1637	Captain John Mason leads colonists to decisive victory in Pequot War.
1638	New Haven Colony established by John Davenport and Theophilus Eaton.
1639	Fundamental Orders of Connecticut adopted by Hartford, Wethersfield, and Windsor; John Haynes chosen first governor.
1643	Connecticut joins in forming the New England Confederation.
1646	New London founded by John Winthrop, Jr.
1650	Code of Laws drawn up by Roger Ludlow and adopted by the legislature.
1662	John Winthrop, Jr., obtains a charter for Connecticut.
1665	Union of New Haven and Connecticut colonies completed.
1675–76	Connecticut participates in King Philip's War.
1687	Edmund Andros assumes rule over Connecticut and Charter Oak episode occurs.
1689	Connecticut resumes government under the charter.
1701	Collegiate School authorized by the General Assembly.
1708	Saybrook Platform, providing more centralized control of the established Congregational Church, approved by the General Assembly.
1717	Collegiate School moves to New Haven and called Yale the next year.
1737	First copper coins in America minted by Samuel Higley of Simsbury.
1740	Manufacture of tinware begun at Berlin by Edward and William Pattison and the beginning of the religious "Great Awakening."

1745	Connecticut troops under Roger Wolcott help capture Louisbourg.
1755	*Connecticut Gazette* of New Haven, the colony's first newspaper, printed by James Parker at New Haven.
1764	*Connecticut Courant*, the oldest American newspaper in continuous existence, launched at Hartford by Thomas Green.
1765	Opposition to the Stamp Act organized by the Sons of Liberty.
1766	Governor Thomas Fitch, who supported the Stamp Act, defeated by William Pitkin.
1767	Thomas and Samuel Green launch newspaper which after many changes in name continues today as the *New Haven Journal-Courier*.
1774	Silas Deane, Eliphalet Dyer, and Roger Sherman represent Connecticut at the First Continental Congress and Connecticut officially extends its jurisdiction over Susquehannah Company area in northern Pennsylvania.
1775	Several thousand militia rush to Massachusetts in the Lexington Alarm; Connecticut men help plan and carry out the seizure of Fort Ticonderoga.
1776	Samuel Huntington, Roger Sherman, William Williams, and Oliver Wolcott sign the Declaration of Independence; large majority of Connecticut people under Governor Jonathan Trumbull support the Declaration of Independence.
1777	British troops under General Tryon raid Danbury.
1779	British troops raid New Haven, Fairfield, Greenwich, Norwalk.
1781	Benedict Arnold's attack upon New London (Fort Trumbull) and Groton (Fort Griswold) involves massacre at Fort Griswold. Washington and Rochambeau confer at Webb House in Wethersfield.
1783	Meeting of Anglican clergy at Glebe House, Woodbury, leads to consecration of Bishop Samuel Seabury and beginning of Protestant Episcopal Church in the United States.
1787	Oliver Ellsworth, William Samuel Johnson, and Roger Sherman serve as Connecticut's representatives at Philadelphia Constitutional Convention.
1788	Convention at Hartford approves Federal Constitution by vote of 128 to 40.

Historic Sites

These selected historic sites are related to the colonial history of Connecticut. There are many other houses built during this period; however, most are not open to the public on a regular basis.

Brooklyn

The nearly square Old Trinity Church has a four-sided hip roof typical of colonial meeting houses.

Coventry

The Nathan Hale Homestead was built in 1776 by Deacon Richard Hale, father of the Patriot, and contains much Hale family memorabilia.

Danbury

The David Taylor House, built in 1750, has a fine collection of Connecticut furniture, clothing, and uniforms.

East Granby

Old Newgate Prison and Copper Mine was used during the Revolutionary War and until 1827 as a prison.

Farmington

The Stanley-Whitman House, an oak clapboard structure of the central-chimney type, was built about 1660 and has diamond-shaped, lead-casement windows. A lean-to addition was added about 1760.

The First Church of Christ, built in 1771 as a meetinghouse, has a slender graceful spire.

Groton

Fort Griswold, on September 6, 1781, was the scene of the massacre by the British forces commanded by Benedict Arnold. The stone fort now houses a Revolutionary War Museum.

Guilford

The oldest stone house in New England and probably in the United States is the Henry Whitfield House, built in 1639 with stone quarried a quarter mile away. It served the early settlers as a fort, church, and meeting hall as well as a home.

The Hyland House was built about 1660 and the Griswold House in 1735.

Hartford

The Wadsworth Atheneum contains the Wallace Nutting Collection of Furniture of the Pilgrim Century (1620–1720) as well as Revolutionary paintings by John Trumbull.

The State Library and Museum has the original charter granted by Charles II and the state constitutions. A full-length portrait of George Washington by Gilbert Stuart and portraits of the governors are on view in Memorial Hall.

A plaque on Charter Oak Street shows the location of the famous Charter Oak.

The First Church of Christ was established in 1636 with Thomas Hooker as its pastor. Hooker and other pioneers are buried in the Old Burying Ground.

Kent

The Sloane-Stanley Museum has a fine collection of early American hand tools and implements and is located on the site of the original ironworks.

Lebanon

"Brother Jonathan" Trumbull's House (1735) and the War Office, which had been Trumbull's store, are restored to their Revolutionary status.

Litchfield

Litchfield is one of the best-preserved eighteenth-century areas in New England. Founded in 1719, Litchfield was an important military supply depot during the Revolutionary War, and its historic district around the Green and along North and South streets has many houses of historical interest. The home of Oliver Wolcott, a signer of the Declaration of Independence, was built in 1753, and the one-room law office of Tapping Reeve became the first law school in America in 1784.

Mystic

The Denison Homestead was occupied by eleven generations of the Denison family from 1717 until 1941, when it was willed to the Denison Society.

New Canaan

The Hanford-Silliman House (1764), built by Stephen Hanford, a weaver and tavern keeper, was later acquired by Joseph Silliman, whose descendents lived in it until 1924.

New Haven

Connecticut Hall, Yale's only surviving pre-Revolutionary building, completed in 1752, is the center of the old Yale campus. Yale University Art Gallery contains colonial exhibits and Revolutionary paintings and miniatures by John Trumbull.

New Haven Colony Historical Society has an excellent library and collection of colonial materials.

The Pardee-Morris House was built in 1680.

Judges' Cave in West Rock Park was the hiding place of Edward Whalley and William Goffe, the famous regicides.

New London

The Hemsted House, built in 1678 by one of the original settlers of the city, is the oldest surviving house in New London to have escaped the burning of that city by Benedict Arnold in 1781.

The Shaw Mansion, built in 1756 by Acadian settlers from Nova Scotia, was one of the places where Washington slept.

Niantic

The Thomas Lee House (1660) is a saltbox and the oldest frame house in Connecticut.

Norwich

The Leffingwell Inn (1675) was turned into a public house in 1700 and served as a stage-stop between Worcester and New London. It became the site of many meetings of the Sons of Liberty, and Washington ate there in 1776.

Redding

The Continental Army under the command of General Israel Putnam spent the winter of 1779 encamped here. Many of the log buildings have been reconstructed and a Revolutionary War Museum is part of the Putnam Memorial Park.

Suffield

The main part of the Hatheway House was built about 1760 and the North Wing in 1795. Under one roof are three different Connecticut architectural styles spanning the eighteenth century as well as fine federal-period furnishings, fine paneling, and original late eighteenth-century French wallpapers.

Wethersfield

The restored Buttolph-Williams House is a fine example of a 1692 colonial frame mansion with a completely furnished kitchen typical of the period.

The Joseph Webb House (1752) still has the original dark-red flock wallpaper in the bedroom where Washington slept in 1781 while he and Count de Rochambeau spent five days planning the Yorktown campaign, which brought an end to the American Revolution.

Silas Deane's House (1766) is located nearby and has an elaborately carved mahogany staircase.

Windsor

The Fyler House is the oldest house (1640) in the oldest town in Connecticut.

Bibliography

Adams, James Truslow, *The Founding of New England*. Vol. I. Boston: Little, Brown, and Company, 1927.
Bacon, Edwin M., *The Connecticut River and the Valley of the Connecticut*. New York: G. P. Putnam's Sons, 1911.
Barrow, Thomas C., *Connecticut Joins the Revolution*. Chester, Conn.: Pequot Press, 1973.
Beals, Carleton, *Our Yankee Heritage, New England's Contribution to American Civilization*. New York: David McKay Company, Inc., 1955.
Black, Robert C., *The Younger John Winthrop*. New York: Columbia University Press, 1966.
Bushman, Richard L., *From Puritan to Yankee: Character and the Social Order in Connecticut, 1690–1765*. New York: W. W. Norton & Company, 1967.
Calder, Isabel MacBeath, *The New Haven Colony*. New Haven, Conn.: Yale University Press, 1934.
Callahan, North, *Connecticut's Revolutionary War Leaders*. Chester, Conn.: Pequot Press, 1973.
Clark, George L., *A History of Connecticut: Its People and Institutions*. New York: G. P. Putnam's Sons, 1914.
Collier, Christopher, *Connecticut in the Continental Congress*. Chester, Conn.: Pequot Press, 1973.
Destler, Chester M., *Connecticut: The Provisions State*. Chester, Conn.: Pequot Press, 1973.
Earle, Alice Morse, *Home Life in Colonial Days*. New York: The Macmillan Company, 1969.
East, Robert A., *Connecticut's Loyalists*. Chester, Conn.: Pequot Press, 1974.
Edmonds, Walter D., *The Musket and the Cross*. Boston: Little, Brown and Company, 1968.
Frost, J. William, *Connecticut Education in the Revolutionary Era*. Chester, Conn.: Pequot Press, 1974.
Gocher, W. H., *Wadsworth or the Charter Oak*. Hartford, Conn.: W. H. Gocher, 1904.
Hall-Quest, Olga, *Flames over New England: The Story of King Philip's War, 1675–1676*. New York: E. P. Dutton & Company, Inc., 1967.
Hard, Walter, *The Connecticut River*. Rivers of America Series. New York: Rinehart and Company, 1947.
Hamilton, Edward P., *The French and Indian War*. Mainstream of America Series. Garden City, N.Y.: Doubleday and Co., Inc., 1962.
Hoyt, Joseph B., *The Connecticut Story*. New Haven, Conn.: Readers Press, Inc., 1961.
Johnston, Alexander, *Connecticut: A Study of a Commonwealth Democracy*. Boston: Houghton, Mifflin and Company, 1903.
Jones, Mary Jeanne Anderson, *Congregational Commonwealth: Connecticut, 1636–1662*. Middletown, Conn.: Wesleyan University Press, 1963.
Leach, Douglas Edward, *Arms for Empire*. New York: Macmillan Company, 1973.

Litchfield Associates, *A Guide to Historic Sites in Connecticut*. Middletown, Conn.: Wesleyan University Press, 1963.
Kelly, J. Frederick, *Connecticut's Old Houses: A Handbook and Guide*. Essex, Conn.: Pequot Press, 1963.
Martin, Joseph Plumb, *Private Yankee Doodle*. George F. Scheer, ed. Boston: Little, Brown and Company, 1962.
McDevitt, Robert, *Connecticut Attacked: A British Viewpoint, Tryon's Raid on Danbury*. Chester, Conn.: Pequot Press, 1974.
McNulty, John Bard, *Older Than the Nation: The Story of the Hartford Courant*. Stonington, Conn.: Pequot Press, 1964.
Miller, John C., *The First Frontier: Life in Colonial America*. New York: Delacorte Press, 1966.
Mills, Lewis Sprague, *The Story of Connecticut*. 5th ed. West Rindge, N.H.: Richard R. Smith Publisher, Inc., 1958.
Morgan, Edmund S., *The Puritan Family, Religion and Domestic Relations in Seventeenth-Century New England*. New York: Harper & Row, 1966.
Morgan, Forrest, ed., *Connecticut as a Colony and as a State, or One of the Original Thirteen*, Vols. I and II. Hartford, Conn.: The Publishing Society of Connecticut, 1904.
Peckham, Howard, *The War for Independence*. Chicago: University of Chicago Press, 1958.
Perry, Charles Edward, ed., *Founders and Leaders of Connecticut, 1633–1783*. Boston: D. C. Heath and Company, 1934.
Phelps, Richard H., *Newgate of Connecticut: Its Origin and Early History*. Hartford, Conn.: American Publishing Company, 1876.
Roth, David M., "Connecticut and the Coming of the Revolution." *The Connecticut Review*, VII: 1 (October 1973).
Roth, David M., *Connecticut's War Governor: Jonathan Trumbull*. Chester, Conn.: Pequot Press, 1974.
Sanford, Elias B., *A History of Connecticut*, rev. ed. Hartford, Conn.: The S. S. Scranton Company, 1922.
Steiner, Bernard C., *The History of Education in Connecticut*. Washington, D.C.: Government Printing Office, 1893.
Tercentenary Commission Pamphlets, I–LX. New Haven, Conn.: Yale University Press, 1933–1936.
Tucker, Louis Leonard, *Connecticut's Seminary of Sedition: Yale College*. Chester, Conn.: Pequot Press, 1974.
Trumbull, Benjamin, *A Complete History of Connecticut: Civil and Ecclesiastical*. New London, Conn.: H. D. Utley, 1898.
Tunis, Edwin, *Colonial Craftsmen*. New York: World Publishing Company, 1965.
Van Dusen, Albert E., *Connecticut*. New York: Random House, 1961.
White, David O., *Connecticut's Black Soldiers: 1775–1783*. Chester, Conn.: Pequot Press, 1973.
Wissler, Clark, *Indians of the United States*, rev. ed. New York: Doubleday & Company, 1966.
Zeichner, Oscar, *Connecticut's Years of Controversy, 1750–1776*. Chapel Hill, N.C.: University of North Carolina Press, 1949.

Index

A

Acadia, capture of, 90
Adultery, punishment of, 60
Algonkian Indians, 10
André, Major John, 134
Andros, Sir Edmund, 70; arrest of, 73; and charter, 70, 71, 73; despotism under, 73
Arnold, Benedict, 129; and attack on New Haven, 129; as British officer, 134; contributions of, 131; at Danbury, 125; early career of, 129; leadership of, 112; military career of, 130; at New London, 134; and Peggy Shippen, 133; at Philadephia, 133; at Quebec, 131; at Saratoga, 133; treason of, 134
Articles of Confederation, 144
Artisan class, growth of, 79

B

Baking, 28
Barter, trade by, 83
Bay Colony, differences with, 29; dislike of life in, 23
Bible State of the New Haven Colony, 44
Bill of Rights, establishment of, 73
Bissell, Israel, 111
Black soldiers, 117
Block, Adriaen, 9, 13; explorations of, 15
Block Island, 15
Boston Tea Party, report of, 109
Boundaries of colony, 64
British raids, 127
Brooke, Lord, 32
Brother Jonathan, meaning of term, 122
Brownists, 20
Buell, Abel, and type founding, 96
Bunker Hill, battle of, 114
Burgoyne, retreat of, 133
Burr, Aaron, at New Haven, 127
Butler, John, 126
Butler, Zebulon, 126

C

Charles II, ascension of, 62
Charter of 1662, 64; end by Andros of, 73; hiding the, 72; petition for, 62; requests for surrender of, 71; restoration of the, 73
Charter Oak, 72
Charters, conflicts in, 69
Cheever, Ezekial, 58
Children, role of, 55
Christiaensen, Hendrick, 13
Church in New Haven, importance of, 44, 45, 46
Church, Dr. Benjamin, 131
Civil liberties, importance of, 52
Climate, 13
Clothing, Indian, 12
Code of 1650, 51; coverage of the, 52
Coins, copper, 82
Collegiate School, charter for, 77
Committee of Correspondence, membership in, 109
Common, importance of town, 48
Community, discipline, 59; life, 48; punishment, 53
Concord, effect of battle of, 111
Conflict, between eastern and western Connecticut, 105; Indian tribal, 10, 11; with Indians, 36; paper money, 106; with Pennsylvania, land, 87; religious, 75
Conflicts, in charters, 69; between England and France, 89; over expansion, 88
Conformity, characteristic of, 61
Congregational Church, 20; disestablishment of, 87; *See also* Puritans.
Connecticut Compromise, 8, 145
Connecticut Courant, founding of, 92, 93; *See also Hartford Courant.*
Connecticut Gazette, 92
Connecticut, Long Island claims of, 70
Connecticut River Valley, 10, 12, 14
Connecticut Yankee, emergence of, 61

155

Constitution, need for federal, 143; ratification of, 145
Constitutional Convention, 144
Constitutions, Fundamental Orders as models for, 31
Continental Congress, delegates to, 109
Cooking, 28
Copper, coins, 82; discovery of, 82; smelting, 82
Cornwallis, surrender of, 138
Cotton, John, 23
Crops, nature of, 78
Crown Point, battle of, 99, 100
Curler, Jacob Van, 17

D

Daggert, Naphtali at New Haven, 127
Danbury, action at, 124; destruction of, 125
Davenport, James, and evangelism, 85
Davenport, John, 39; departure for Connecticut of, 43; departure from England of, 42; nonconformism of, 42; and regicides, 65
Deane, Silas, 109
Decentralization of Connecticut, 61
Declaration of Independence, 117
Desertion of troops, 114
Dieskau, Baron Ludwig August, 97
Discipline, community, 59; family, 55
Distribution of land, 47
Divorce, 61
Dixwell, John, 66
Doolittle, Isaac, and printing presses, 96
Dutch settlements, 16
Dyer, Eliphalet, 109

E

Eastern and western Connecticut, conflict between, 105
Easterners, power of, 107
Eaton, Theophilus, 42; ambitions of, 42; government power of, 46
Economy, postwar, 140; strength of Connecticut, 101
Education, compulsory, 58; importance of, 58
Edwards, Rev. Jonathan, and religious revival, 85
Eliot, Rev. John, and Indian missions, 66
Elizabeth I, reign of, 20
Ellsworth, Oliver, 8; and Constitutional Convention, 144
Endicott, John, raids of, 37
England, debts of, 101; dissatisfaction with policies of, 92; explorations sponsored by, 19; and France, conflicts between, 89; after French and Indian War, 101; growth of power of, 20; newspapers and relations with, 93; religious reform in, 19, 20
English, merchant marine, growth of, 20; settlement, 17; taxation, resistance to, 102
Expansion, conflicts over, 88
Expansionists, power of, 108

F

Family, discipline, 55; Puritan, 53; size, 55
Farm lands, productivity decrease of, 87
Farming, inefficiency of, 78; suitability of land for, 78; tools, 80
Farmington, settlement of, 48
Father, role of the Puritan, 55
Fenwick, George, activities of, 50; return to England of, 50; settlement of, 49
Figurative Map, 16
Fireplace, importance of the, 27, 28
Fitch, Thomas, downfall of, 107; early career of, 106; and taxation protest, 102
Food, rivers as a source of, 12; supplies, wartime, 116
Forests, 13
Fort Griswold, massacre at, 136; See also Groton.
Fort Saybrook, 32; construction of, 34; sale of, 50
Fort William Henry, 98
Forty Fort, defeat at, 126
France and England, conflicts between, 89
French and Indian War, 96; changes in status of, 100; effect on Connecticut of, 101; end of, 100
Fundamental Orders, acceptance of, 31; as constitutional model, 31; government under the, 31; writing of the, 30
Fur trade, 10, 16

G

Gardiner, David, birth of, 35
Gardiner, Lion, 34, 35
Gardiner's Island, 49
Gates, Major General Horatio, 132
General Court of the Three River Towns, 29
Glorious Revolution and James II, 73
Goffe, William, 65
Goodwin, George, 94
Goodyear, Stephen, and iron foundries, 82
Government changes, postwar, 140
Grain mills, 80
Great Awakening, 85
Green, Thomas, and *Connecticut Courant*, 93
Green, Timothy, and *New London Gazette*, 93; and *New London Summary*, 93
Groton, destruction of, 134, 135, 136; See also Fort Griswold.
Gun supplies, wartime, 122

156

H

Hairstyles, Indian, 12
Hale, Nathan, early life of, 117; enlistment of, 118; execution of, 119; spying activities of, 118
Half-way Covenant, terms of, 75
Hartford, growth of, 27; settlement at, 17, 24
Hartford Courant, history of, 92; See also *Connecticut Courant*.
Haynes, John, 23; election as governor, 32
Hempstead, Stephen, 118
Higginson, Rev. John, and first school, 58
Higley, Joseph, and steel manufacture, 82
Holmes, William, settlement of, 17
Hooker, Thomas, 21; conflict over, 22, 23; departure to Holland, 23; departure for New England, 23; early career of, 22; move to Connecticut, 24, 25; political ideas of, 30; political sermon of, 30
Housatonic River, 12
House of Hope, departure from, 18; establishment of, 17
Houses, description of early, 27; heating, 28
Howe, General, action at Danbury, 124
Hudson, Barzillai, and *Connecticut Courant*, 94
Hudson, Henry, influence of, 13
Huntington, Samuel, 143, 144

I

Independence of Connecticut, 65
Indian, attacks, 68; clothing, 12; conflict, tribal, 10, 11, 30; hairstyles, 12; land sales, 17; life, 11; missions and John Eliot, 66; raids, 100; slavery, 84; tribes, 10
Indians, Algonkian, 10; conflict with, 36; and New Haven Colony, 44; raids against, 37; relations with, 67; River Valley, 11
Ingersoll, Jared, career of, 102; resignation as stamp tax collector, 104; as stamp tax collector, 103
Iron industry, 81, 82

J

James II, ascension of, 70; and the Glorious Revolution, 73; New England plans of, 71
Johnson, William, and the Constitutional Convention, 144; and the French and Indian War, 97

K

Kievet's Hook, 17
King George's War, 90

King Philip, death of, 69; war of, 66, 69
King William's War, 89

L

Lake George, battle of, 97
Land, distribution of, 47; purchases, English, 17; sales, Indian, 17
Land of Steady Habits, nickname, 61
Laud, William, opposition to Hooker of, 22
Law, equal protection of the, 52
Laws, code of, 51
Ledyard, William, at Fort Griswold, 136
Leete, Andrew and the charter, 71
Lexington, effect of battle of, 111
Long Island Sound, 12
Louisbourg, attack on, 91
Ludlow, Roger, 30; and code of laws, 52; election as deputy governor, 32
Lyman, Phineas, in French and Indian War, 97

M

Map, Figurative, 16
Martin, Joseph Plumb, war descriptions of, 115, 125
Mason, John, 39
Massachusetts. See Bay Colony.
Mecom, Benjamin, and *Connecticut Gazette*, 93
Meetinghouse, design of the, 56; role of the, 56
Merchant marine, growth of English, 20
Metacomet. See King Philip.
Migrations from Connecticut, postwar, 141
Milford, settlement of, 47
Militia, contribution of Connecticut, 115; desertion of, 114; mobilization for Revolution of, 112
Mills, grain, 80
Millwheels, types of, 81
Ministers, power of the, 58
Mr. Ludlow's Code, 52
Money, conflict over paper, 106; first paper, 90; for Revolution, raising, 112
Montcalm, Louis Joseph Marquis de, 100

N

Naugatuck river, 12
New England Confederation, formation of, 50; function of, 51
New England Society for Trade and Commerce, 106
Newgate Prison, 119; escapes from, 120
New Haven, battle of, 127; church importance in, 44, 45, 46; government of, 44; government and Eaton, 46; green, layout of, 44; and Indians, 44; integration into

157

Connecticut, 65; layout of, 44; settlement of, 43; Seven Pillars, 44; theocracy in, 46
New Haven Colony, Bible State of the, 44; flight of the, 41; War, 29
New Lights, 86
New London, Arnold attack on, 129; destruction of, 134, 135, 136
New London Gazette, 93
New London Summary, 93
Newman, Francis, 44
Newspapers, content of, 94; role of, 93
New York, claims to Connecticut of, 69, 70
Nickname, Land of Steady Habits, 61
Nova Scotia, attack on, 91

O

Occupations, varieties of, 78
Oldham, John, 24; murder of, 37
Old Lights, 86
Onrust, 9, 14

P

Paper, availability of, 96; money, conflict over, 106; money, issuance of first, 90
Parker, James, and *Connecticut Gazette,* 92
Pattison, Edward, and tinware, 82
Pattison, William, and tinware, 82
Peddlers, growth of Yankee, 82, 83
Pennsylvania, land conflict with, 87; migration to, 108; settlers, problems of, 126
Pepperrell, William, and Nova Scotia attack, 91
Pequot Indians, 10
Pilgrims, 20
Pillory, use of the, 60
Pitkin, William, as governor, 107
Plantation covenant of New Haven, 44
Political, stability, 88; unity, end of, 88
Population, increase, 87; patterns, changes in, 74; problems, postwar, 141; study of, 109
Postwar, changes, 139, 140; issues, 139
Presbyterians, 20
Printing, equipment, 95; industry, 96
Printshops, role of the, 95
Prudden, Rev. Peter, 46; departure from New Haven of, 47
Publishing, printers' role in, 95
Punishment, community, 53
Puritan, family, 53; method of settlement, 47; rule, end of, 62; standards, 53; standards, decline of, 74
Puritans, 20; general picture of, 53
Putnam, Israel, 112; death of, 125; early career of, 113; importance of, 114
Putnam, Rufus, migration to Ohio of, 141

Q

Quebec, Arnold at, 131
Queen Anne's War, 89

R

Raids against Indians, 37
Rations, wartime allocation of, 116
Recruitment problems, wartime, 117
Regicides, 65
Regional differences, 139
Religion, postwar change in, 140
Religious, conflict, 75, 86; conflict, English, 19; reformers, English, 20; revival, 85; revival and Jonathan Edwards, 85; services, 57
River Valley Indians, 11
Rivers, importance of, 12; major, 12
Rogers, Robert, and French and Indian War, 100
Russell, Rev. John, and regicides, 66

S

Sabbath, importance of the, 57
Saltonstall, Gurdon, 75
Saratoga, battle of, 133
Sassacus, description of, 36, 37
Sawmill, importance of, 81
Say and Sele, Lord, 32
Saybrook, growth of, 50
Saybrook Company, formation of, 32
Saybrook Platform, adoption of, 75
Schools, establishment of, 58
Self-government, 64
Separatists, 20
Servants, role of, 56
Settlement, Puritan method of, 47
Settlements, Dutch, 16
Seven Pillars of New Haven, 44
Shay's Rebellion, 143
Sherman, Roger, 8, 109; career of, 142; and Constitutional Convention, 144; public service of, 142
Shipbuilding industry, 82
Shippen, Peggy, and Benedict Arnold, 134
Shirley, William, and French and Indian War, 97; and Nova Scotia attack, 91
Simsbury copper mines, 82; prison use of, 120
Sizing and land distribution, 47
Slave, soldiers, 117; trade, 84
Slavery, abolition of, 140; acceptance of, 84; in Connecticut, 56
Slaves, role of, 85
Smith, Captain John, explorations of, 15
Society of Cincinnati, opposition to, 139
Soldiers, problem of the summer, 115
Sons of Liberty, activities of, 109; power of, 107; and taxation opposition, 103, 104

Spenser, Joseph, 112
Stamp Act, 101; and Jared Ingersoll, 103; and Sons of Liberty, 103, 104
Stanley, Nathaniel, and the charter, 72
Steel manufacture and Joseph Higley, 82
Steele, John, 24
Stiles, Ezra, 129
Stone, Captain John, murder of, 37
Stone, Samuel, 23
Stone Age Indian life, 12
Sugar Act, 101
Summer soldiers, problem of the, 115
Susquehannah Company, 87; revival of, 108

T

Talcott, John, 64
Taxation, of colonies, reasons for, 101; resistance to English, 102
Taxes during Revolutionary War, 112
Ten Adventurers, The, 24
Thames river, 12
Theocracy in New Haven, 44
Thomas, Isaiah, account of Lexington and Concord, 112
Three River Towns, General Court of the, 29; government of the, 31; settlement of the, 24. See also Hartford, Wethersfield, Windsor.
Tinware and Pattison brothers, 82
Tories, reconciliation with, 139
Tory sympathizers, 124; persecution of, 110
Townshend Duties, 101; opposition to, 109
Trade, by barter, 83; increase in, 16, 83
Transportation, improvement in, 83; river, 12
Treat, Robert, and the charter, 71; reelection as governor, 73
Treaty of Paris, 100
Tribes, Indian, 10
Trumbull family, contributions of, 123
Trumbull, Jonathan, career of, 121; election of, 107; wartime activities of, 115, 122
Tryon, William, and Danbury, 124; raids of, 127
Twiller, Wouter Van, 17

U

United New Netherland Company, the, 15

V

Veterans' benefits, 139
Victory, celebration of, 138

W

Wadsworth, Joseph, and hiding charter, 72
Walley, Edward, 65
Walloons, Belgian, 16
War effort, contribution to the, 115
War, Pequot, 39
Warwick Patent, 33, 50, 63
Washington, George, in Connecticut, 136
Waterpower, river, 12
Watson, Ebenezer, 112; and *Connecticut Courant,* 94
Watson, Hannah, and *Connecticut Courant,* 94
Weekly Advertiser. See *New London Summary.*
Western Connecticut, Tories in, 124
Western and eastern Connecticut, conflicts between, 105
Wethersfield, growth of, 27; settlement of, 24
Whitefield, George, and evangelism, 85, 86
Wigwams, 12
William and Mary, rule of, 73
Windsor, establishment of, 18; growth of, 27
Winslow, Edward, land purchase of, 17
Winthrop, Fitz-John, 77
Winthrop, John, Jr., and charter petition, 63; description of, 63; and iron foundries, 81
Wolcott, Roger, and Nova Scotia attack, 91
Women in Puritan society, role of, 53
Woopigwooit, Chief, 17; murder of, 36
Wooster, David, 112
Wyllys, Samuel, 64
Wyoming Massacre, 126
Wyoming Valley, problems of settlers in, 126

Y

Yale College, graduates of, 78; naming of, 78
Yankee peddlers, growth of, 82, 83
Yorktown, surrender at, 138